PETER LETKEMANN,
author of this volume,
is Assistant Professor of Sociology
at the University of Lethbridge,
Alberta, Canada.

CRIME
AS
WORK

Peter Letkemann

Prentice-Hall, Inc. *Englewood Cliffs, N.J.*

Library of Congress Cataloging in Publication Data

LETKEMANN, PETER.
  Crime as work.

  (A Spectrum Book)
  Bibliography: p.
  1. Crime and criminals.   2. Criminal psychology.
3. Work—Psychological aspects.   I. Title.
HV6025.L46   364'.023   73–12071
ISBN   0–13–192914–3
ISBN   0–13–192922–4 (pbk.)

10   9   8   7   6   5   4   3   2   1

PRENTICE-HALL INTERNATIONAL, INC. (*London*)
PRENTICE-HALL OF AUSTRALIA PTY. LTD. (*Sydney*)
PRENTICE-HALL OF CANADA LTD. (*Toronto*)
PRENTICE-HALL OF INDIA PRIVATE LIMITED (*New Delhi*)
PRENTICE-HALL OF JAPAN, INC. (*Tokyo*)

To my respondents,
particularly Bob and Lloyd,
who so generously shared
their experiences with me

CONTENTS

CONTENTS

ACKNOWLEDGMENTS

To my respondents, for their cooperation and helpfulness;

To Professors Adrian Marriage and Roy Turner,
who alerted me to sociological implications of my work;

To The Canadian Penitentiary Service, for interviewing privileges;

To The Canada Council, for financial support.

Thank you.

1

INTRODUCTION

We usually get our car the night before, and we naturally check over our weapons . . . usually if we're gonna meet in the morning we just sort of casually saunter into a coffee shop, just like the working stiff, you know—have a cup of coffee.

This is a book about crime and those who think of it as their work. It is intended as an addition to that small yet growing body of research that describes and analyses criminal behavior. Particular emphasis is given to the technical and organizational dimensions of such behavior. The value of such an emphasis derives partly from the tendency of researchers to bypass these dimensions in favor of research on characteristics of the criminal and on the ways in which official agencies come to define certain persons as being criminals. Although these latter approaches are not to be discounted, sociologists have argued that very little is actually known about criminal behavior, despite the magnitude of the literature, both scientific and journalistic, on crime. Much has been inferred from the illegitimacy of crime, but little from the behavior itself. The pervasiveness of the crime theme in the popular media obscures the fact that information about what criminals do, their methods of operation, careers, life styles and relationships with each other, is limited and fragmented.

In 1955, David Maurer, a linguist specializing in criminal argot, commented:

1

Actually we know little about crime as a way of life; in fact, we have more data on the behavior pattern of almost any obscure primitive tribe than we have on these problem areas within our own culture. . . .[1]

Complaints regarding the scarcity of descriptive material on criminal behavior are still to be found in many criminology texts and related publications. Wolfgang and Ferracuti, who subtitled their work "Towards an Integrated Theory in Criminology," state:

Unfortunately, there has thus far been inadequate attention and research time given to a full description and analysis of criminal offence types.[2]

The continued use of studies such as Sutherland's *The Professional Thief*,[3] Whyte's *Street-Corner Society*[4] and Thrasher's *The Gang*,[5] with publication dates of 1937, 1943, and 1927 respectively, indicates not only their academic value but also the relative absence of comparable, contemporary research.

Other early descriptive studies that continue to influence the study of crime, include Maurer's *The Big Con*[6] and *Whiz Mob*,[7] W. I. Thomas's *The Unadjusted Girl*,[8] Shaw's *The Jack-Roller*,[9] Jerome Hall's *Theft, Law and Society*,[10] and Donald Cressey's *Other People's Money*.[11] The subsequent proliferation of studies based on a generally uncritical usage of official statistics was not theoretically

1. David Maurer, *Whiz Mob* (New Haven, Conn.: College and University Press, 1964).
2. M. E. Wolfgang and F. Ferracuti, *The Subculture of Violence* (London: Tavistock Publications, 1967), p. 40.
3. Edwin Sutherland, *The Professional Thief* (Chicago: University of Chicago Press, 1937).
4. W. F. Whyte, *Street-Corner Society* (Chicago: University of Chicago Press, 1943).
5. F. M. Thrasher, *The Gang: A Study of 1313 Gangs in Chicago* (Chicago: University of Chicago Press, 1927).
6. Maurer, *The Big Con* (Indianapolis: The Bobbs-Merrill Co., Inc., 1940).
7. Maurer, *Whiz Mob*. First published by the American Dialect Society, Gainesville, Florida, in 1955.
8. W. I. Thomas, *The Unadjusted Girl* (Boston: Little, Brown and Company, 1923).
9. C. Shaw, *The Jack-Roller* (Chicago: University of Chicago Press, 1930).
10. Jerome Hall, *Theft, Law and Society* (Indianapolis: The Bobbs-Merrill Co., Inc., 1952).
11. D. R. Cressey, *Other People's Money: A Study of the Social Psychology of Embezzlement* (Glencoe, Ill.: The Free Press, 1953).

productive; telling us, as Maurer puts it ". . . a little (a very little) about the criminal, a good deal about the investigator and his methods, and almost nothing about crime." [12] The work of other writers and journalists who have dealt in more popular styles with the subject, and whose material has been used frequently for supplementing academic research, has been helpful.

The dearth of descriptive material dealing specifically and analytically with criminal behavior may be accounted for partly by the inaccessability of such data, as opposed to the ease of obtaining statistical data. Because of its illegitimacy, practitioners have an interest in maintaining secrecy.[13] Writers and journalists, even those who have found entrance into criminal subcultures, find it necessary to fill in or embellish their otherwise incomplete accounts. In addition, researchers interested in communicating directly with confined criminals will probably find that the prison administration makes the prisoner's file more accessible than the prisoner.

Until about 1965, sociologists theorizing about crime have had to rely almost exclusively on a few early studies for descriptive and analytic information. More recently, the literature indicates a shift in the direction of research. A serious look at the categories that constitute official statistics has resulted in several descriptive accounts having to do with the processes of official decision-making.[14] Contemporary interest in the styles of Sutherland and Maurer is evident. W. J. Eistadter,[15] in his study of the social organization of armed robbery, examines his data with references to Sutherland's work. He concludes that the contemporary style of armed robbery bears little resemblance to the professionalism described by Sutherland. Similar in style to Sutherland's autobiography, is the account by Williamson, edited by R. Lincoln Keiser,[16] and Bruce Jackson's

12. Maurer, *Whiz Mob*, p. 12.

13. Ned Polsky has argued that the difficulty of doing research on illegitimate behavior is greatly exaggerated but agrees that a real consequence of the exaggeration is that researchers have preferred to do research on the "law side" of crime. See Polsky, *Hustlers, Beats and Others* (Chicago: Aldine Publishing Company, 1967), chap. 3.

14. David Sudnow, "Normal Crimes: Sociological Features of the Penal Code," *Social Problems* 12 (Winter 1965): 255–70. Aaron Cicourel, *The Social Organization of Juvenile Justice* (New York: John Wiley & Sons Inc., 1968). J. Skolnik, *Justice Without Trial* (New York: John Wiley & Sons Inc., 1966).

15. W. J. Eistadter, "The Social Organization of Armed Robbery," *Social Problems* 17, no. 1 (Summer 1969): 64–83.

16. H. Williamson, *Hustler!*, R. Lincoln Keiser, ed. (New York: Avon Books, 1965). In his concluding commentary, Bohannan states, "Indeed, not since

A Thief's Primer.[17] In 1965, Gibbons pointed out that we are just beginning to gather data on the question "What do delinquents do?".[18] In the same vein, Camp, in his study of bank robbery, points out that his ". . . main unit of analysis moves away from the actor (the bank robber) to the action (the robbery) . . .",[19] and Polsky (1967) applies an occupational perspective to his study of poolroom hustling.[20]

It is my intention, therefore, as stated earlier, to add to that growing body of research that describes and analyses criminal behavior. An effort will be made to get as close to such activity as possible, by way of extensive use of verbatim accounts by criminals.

Not only in the sociology of crime but in other fields as well we have often studied the implications of behavior before studying the behavior itself. Implications of industrialization were studied at great length prior to any detailed examinations of behavior within industry. General worker dissatisfaction was inferred prior to recognition of variations *within* industry.

> Only recently has there been reborn an interest in the core feature of the modern industrial world—the technologies upon which it is grounded.[21]

Case studies of factory work have paid off theoretically. Sweeping generalizations have been replaced because of a new appreciation of variations within industry.

As indicated, particular attention will be focused upon the technical and organizational dimensions of criminal behavior. It is reasonable to assume that criminal behavior should be no less immune to the effects of technological change than noncriminal behavior. Nowhere, to my knowledge, have the effects of technological change (for example, unemployment, worker retraining, specialization) been studied with reference to criminal behavior. As with early

Sutherland's 'Professional Thief' forty years ago have we had so full an account from the other side of the law."

17. Bruce Jackson, *A Thief's Primer* (New York: The Macmillan Company, 1969).

18. D. C. Gibbons, *Changing the Lawbreaker: The Treatment of Delinquents and Criminals* (Englewood Cliffs, N.J.: Prentice-Hall, Inc., 1965), p. 385.

19. G. M. Camp, "Nothing to Lose: A Study of Bank Robbery in America" (Ph.D. diss., Yale University, 1967), p. iii.

20. Polsky, *Hustlers, Beats and Others.*

21. R. Dubin, et al., *Leadership and Productivity* (San Francisco: Chandler Publishing Co., 1965), p. 10.

studies of industrialization, studies of crime have been characterized by generalizations. David Maurer recognizes that criminal techniques vary over time, but insists on the continuity of underlying principles.[22]

Although Maurer himself spells out the principles of confidence games and demonstrates their applicability over time, no such principles are available for other types of crime. It is clear from Maurer's own studies, that such principles cannot be developed without a detailed knowledge of technique. Such knowledge is unavailable for most major crimes, except in bits and pieces. For an example of the utility of Maurer's principles, we must refer again to his own work. He quotes the psychiatrist Gregory Zilboorg, who had accounted for the fact that pickpockets like to "work" the crowds who watched the public hangings of criminals in terms of the pickpockets having "vicariously participated in the act of execution . . . had vicariously paid for past sins . . . then proceeded to pick pockets [as] revenge for their vicarious execution." [23] Maurer is critical of this explanation:

> But if he had even a rudimentary understanding of how pickpockets live and work, he would never have made the statement just quoted. He does not know that the timing of theft from the person can be easily explained on the basis of a very sound mechanical principle of misdirection which is as old as organized thievery. "You can't steal a man's money as long as he has his mind on it." [24]

The "mechanical principle of misdirection" referred to by Maurer places the criminal within the context of the sane and the rational, rather than the pathological and possibly bizarre. The principle of misdirection seems to be an extension and refinement of a principle used by many noncriminals for legitimate purposes. More important, the simpler and therefore preferred interpretation of the act requires a thorough knowledge of criminal technique, or as Sudnow[25] might put it, of the "procedural basis" of criminal behavior. Attention to the technical and organizational aspects of criminal behavior places such research within the rubric of the sociology of

---

22. Maurer, *Whiz Mob*, p. 14.
23. Maurer, *Whiz Mob*, pp. 14–15, quoting Gregory Zilboorg, *The Psychology of the Criminal Act and Punishment* (New York: Harcourt Brace Jovanovich 1954), pp. 65–66.
24. Maurer, *Whiz Mob*, pp. 14–15.
25. D. Sudnow, *Passing On* (Englewood Cliffs, N.J.: Prentice-Hall, Inc., 1967).

work and occupations. For example, both criminals and noncriminals need to develop certain skills necessary for the successful completion of work tasks. Furthermore, the temporal dimensions of work place certain restraints upon nonwork time. The implication of technology and of work time has been studied in considerable detail by sociologists of work and industry. What I am suggesting is that the various dimensions of work appear to be as applicable, for the purposes of study, to the illegitimate as to the legitimate worker. Such an approach will draw attention to the similarities as well as the differences between crime as work and ordinary work.

Ned Polsky applied the concepts, both of the sociology of work and the sociology of leisure, to his study on poolroom hustlers. Although the study itself is a strong case for the continued application of this approach, he has argued his position more explicitly.

> Criminologists stand to lose little and gain much in the way of sociological understanding if, when studying people dedicated to an illegal occupation, they will overcome their fascination with the "illegal" part long enough to focus on the "occupation" part. After all, any theory of illegal occupations can be but a special case, albeit an important one, of general occupational theory.
>
> Criminologists, following the lead of the late Edwin Sutherland, recognize that one hallmark of the career criminal—be he engaged in major crime or, like the hustler most of the time, in violating generally unenforced criminal law—is that the illegal activity in question constitutes his regular job. Yet their researches seem thoroughly untenanted by what occupational sociologists have learned about how to look at someone else's regular job.[26]

The potential analytic utility of an occupational perspective in the study of crime may be demonstrated by the examples given below.

My own data on safecracking indicate that safecrackers open safes on a sporadic and irregular schedule. Only in exceptional circumstances would safecrackers attempt to "go on a caper" [27] more often than once a week, despite the fact that profitable opportunities are not seriously reduced by more frequent activity. Traditional explanations for the sporadic activities of criminals have revolved about the need for criminals to restrain their activities periodically in

---

26. Polsky, *Hustlers, Beats and Others*, p. 101.
27. The word "caper" is used by criminals to refer specifically to criminal work.

order to "cool" police "heat," and about the assumption that criminal activity pays so well that its practitioners need only work periodically. These explanations are not to be discounted, yet both raise additional questions. Why do safecrackers not avoid police pressure by moving from city to city rather than by temporarily ceasing activity? Why do safecrackers not accumulate capital by more frequent activity, as would be consistent with the Western capitalist tradition?

An occupational perspective suggests an unusual explanation: namely, that we might be dealing here with a case of "restricted output." Sociologists of work have discovered that the restriction of output is not necessarily due to external factors, but is frequently one of the products of work-group pressure.[28]

> Certainly it is hard to think of occupations in which there is no group preoccupation with definition of proper levels of effort and product and of those levels which, since they may encourage others in the work drama to expect too much, are potentially dangerous for all who share the fate of living by the given trade or calling.[29]

This perspective encourages us to look beyond obvious external restraints (such as police activity), to the implications of being involved in group criminal activity as opposed to operating as a loner. As a second example of the utility of occupational concepts, I refer to Polsky's study of poolroom hustlers.[30] Polsky suggests that ". . . many of the data criminologists refer to by rubrics such as "the occasional criminal" or "occasional crime" would be more sharply conceptualized and better understood under the heading "crime as moonlighting." Referring to studies in industrial sociology, he notes that

> . . . "the industries in which moonlighters found their second jobs were typically those providing opportunities for part-time work." Most crime fits these descriptions perfectly. Indeed, one of the most genuinely appealing things about crime to career criminals and part-timers alike —though one would hardly gather this from criminology texts—is that for most crimes the working hours are both short and flexible.[31]

28. Donald Roy, "Quota Restriction and Goldbricking in a Machine Shop," *American Journal of Sociology* 57 (March 1952): 427–42.
29. E. C. Hughes, "The Sociological Study of Work: An Editorial Forward," *American Journal of Sociology* 57, no. 5 (March 1952): 426.
30. Polsky, *Hustlers, Beats and Others*, p. 103.
31. Ibid.

Skipper and McCaghy's studies of the occupational aspects of being a stripper provide a third and more recent example in the sociology of deviant behavior. By looking at the work-related aspects of being a stripper,[32] these researchers are able to account for what appear to be high rates of lesbianism among strippers, without recourse to psychopathology. Their analysis of the stripper's work-related situation indicates that it is ". . . differentially favorable to the occurrence of homosexual contacts and self concepts." Persons in deviant roles, no less than those who do what is socially approved, are subject to the influence and shaping of various work-related factors and contingencies. These factors, however, will remain hidden unless we deliberately apply to the illegitimate, the perspectives and methods of analysis which we commonly employ to make sense of the legitimate.

In addition, the occupational perspective provides a wide framework within which to analyse the transmission of values and skills, as well as the process and context of learning. Howard Becker has used this framework in his analysis of both the subculture of jazz musicians and the learning of marijuana smoking.[33] James Bryan has documented the learning process of prostitution in terms of the concept of career.[34]

In his response to Merton's theory of differential opportunity[35] in 1938, Cloward pointed out that access to illegitimate means towards success are also differentially distributed.[36] Just as in legitimate careers, those who wish to take illegitimate routes find that access is restricted to those with the requisite background and skills. What is the nature of these skills? How are they learned and taught? In what ways do prisons serve as schools of crime?

These are only some of the troubling and recurring questions of

32. J. K. Skipper and C. H. McCaghy, "Lesbian Behavior as an Adaptation to the Occupation of Stripping," *Social Problems* 17, no. 2 (Fall 1969): 263; also J. K. Skipper and C. H. McCaghy, "Strip-teasers: The Anatomy and Career Contingencies of a Deviant Occupation," *Social Problems* 17, no. 3 (Winter 1970): 391–405.

33. H. S. Becker, *Outsiders* (New York: The Free Press, 1963).

34. J. Bryan, "Apprenticeships in Prostitution," *Social Problems* 12, no. 3 (Winter 1965): 278–97.

35. R. K. Merton, "Social Structure and Anomie," *American Sociological Review* 3 (October 1938): 672–82.

36. Richard Cloward, "Illegitimate Means, Anomie and Deviant Behaviour," *American Sociological Review* 24 (April 1959).

concern to both layman and academic.[37] The work perspective requires that familiar questions be given an unusual focus. How are the concepts of training, unemployment, and specialization applicable to persons in illegitimate trades? What do criminals do in the face of technological change? How specialized are criminals, and how is such specialization developed?

Sociology—certainly, the sociology of occupations—has benefited greatly by the concomitant use of two methodological stances, namely, attention to both behavior and social action. Besides detailed attention to the behavioral dimensions of crime, this study takes seriously the perspective of the criminal himself. This requires that the researcher avoid imposing an "outside" order upon the data. He must find and analyse the categories that are meaningful to the participant. He must look to the actor for answers to questions having to do with the meaning of his actions and their motivations.[38] We have learned, for example, that a purely economic model of man does not adequately explain variations in work behavior and job satisfaction in legitimate industry. The data presented here indicate that this is also true for those in illegitimate work, and that the criminal, like the conventional worker, is motivated in part by the rewards inherent in craftsmanship, expertise, and associated status.

The relationship between the subjective perspective of the actor and its behavioral dimensions poses particular methodological problems for the researcher of criminal behavior. (A brief appendix on methodology is included at the end of this book.) Since the behavior he is studying is illegitimate, there are various and obvious reasons why he is dependent upon the actor for a description of the behavior. This description may be supplemented by persons who become involved in the behavior through circumstance (for example, robbery victims) or through occupation (for example, the police). For details of the procedures and skills involved one must, however,

37. The work perspective, requiring detailed description and analysis of crime, also poses an ethical question, namely, will the information be used for illegitimate purposes? The discussion to follow should assure the reader that crime is not likely to be taught by way of academic analysis.

38. For a sensitive account of how criminals view their prison and parole experiences, see John Irwin, *The Felon* (Englewood Cliffs, N.J.: Prentice-Hall, Inc., 1970).

rely heavily upon the actor's own account, the behavior in question not being amenable to observation without participation.[39]

Sociologists of occupations have pointed out how the demand characteristics of various occupations shape, and are shaped by, the perspective of the worker. Some of the occupational demands of central importance to the worker are largely hidden from the view of the outsider.[40] Detailed examination of such demands is required in order to make intelligible both the perspective and behavior of the worker.[41] This is not to suggest, however, that occupational demands are to be treated only as independent variables—they too may be subject to change in response to the expectations and qualifications the worker brings with him.

It is the objective of this study to see whether considerations of this kind help to make criminal behavior more intelligible. There is also reason to believe that the study of criminal behavior may help to make noncriminal behavior more intelligible. Following from the work of theorists such as Simmel and Schutz is a growing recognition that everyday taken-for-granted routines are legitimate subject matter for sociological analysis, and that it is there, in fact, where one looks for the foundations of social structure. It is also recognized that the taken-for-granted is least obvious to those most intimately acquainted with it. Like the "civilian," [42] the criminal operates on the basis of "background expectancies."

> The member of the society uses background expectancies as a scheme
> of interpretation. With their use actual appearances are for him
> recognizable and intelligible as the appearances-of-familiar-events.
> Demonstrably he is at a loss to tell us specifically of what the ex-

39. The methodological implications will be discussed in the Appendix. It might be noted here that such observational problems are not confined to the study of criminal behavior. Skolnik, in his study of police behavior, discovered that observation was impossible without considerable participation in the behavior to be observed. The methodological implications are similar: the researcher is both observer and actor; the practical consequences are different: Skolnik did not become a criminal through participation, as would the researcher-participant in crime.

40. An excellent example of such an occupation is that of the apartment-house janitor. See Ray Gold, "Janitors versus Tenants: A Status-Income Dilemma," *American Journal of Sociology* 57, no. 5 (March 1952): 486–93.

41. Skolnik, for example, in *Justice Without Trial*, accounts for the often unorthodox behavior of police in terms of the demands of a highly bureaucratized and unresponsive law enforcement organizational structure.

42. The term "civilian," used by criminals to refer to noncriminals (police excepted), will be used throughout for that same purpose.

pectancies consist. When we ask him about them he has little or nothing to say.

For these background expectancies to come into view one must either be a stranger to the "life as usual" character of everyday scenes, or become estranged from them. As Alfred Schutz pointed out, a "special motive" is required to make them problematic. In the sociologist's case this "special motive" consists in the programmatic task of treating a societal member's practical circumstances, which include from the member's point of view the morally necessary character of many of its background features, as matters of theoretical interest.[43]

The nature of "background expectancies" makes possible the documentation of several perspectives. The researcher who is a stranger to the life of crime may be sensitive to what the criminal takes for granted. In turn, the criminal (who, if not a stranger to civilian life, has at least a "special motive" to make the background expectancies of the civilian problematic) may provide new perspectives from which to view the larger legitimate social order.

In this chapter, I have demonstrated the need for descriptive research having to do with the sociology of crime. In briefly summarizing the substantive nature of related literature, I have noted that the prevailing emphases have bypassed the analysis of criminal behavior in favor of the study of criminals and official processes. My argument for descriptive analysis is borne out by Dubin's discussion of the need for description in the development of models and theoretical schemes.

I cannot emphasize too strongly that there is a fundamental place for accurate description in any science. Description, as I have already indicated in the previous chapters, provides the input for developing units of a theory, its laws of interaction, the system states, and the boundaries of the model. Without adequate description, we would not have models that connect with the world that man perceives and about which he theorizes.[44]

Description, other than that of attitudes and behavior, has been limited to that having a direct bearing on behavior; for example, the description of bank architecture is important to us only insofar

43. H. Garfinkel, *Studies in Ethnomethodology* (Englewood Cliffs, N.J.: Prentice-Hall, Inc., 1967), p. 37.
44. R. Dubin, *Theory Building* (New York: The Free Press, 1969), p. 227.

as it helps to explain the behavior of persons involved in a bank robbery. As Brown has said:

> In a work of social science the descriptions of the appearance of things are similarly justified by the connection between appearances and social behavior.[45]

Throughout this chapter I have claimed that my approach will "make more intelligible," "account for," and "help us to understand" the various phenomena to be discussed. Such claims make it reasonable for the reader to expect answers to various "why" as well as "how" questions.

Brown asserts that at each point in an account, it is:

> . . . possible and reasonable to interject the question "why this?"
> . . . No account could give the answers to all such questions: their number would be indefinitely large since each answer could produce a further question. But an account which satisfied no such queries would be a monstrosity, since we should not know which events were responsible for the occurrence of other events.[46]

It is unlikely the queries dealt with here will necessarily satisfy various theoretical concerns. For example, the answer to the question, "Why is the timing of an urban bank robbery less predictable than a rural one?" appears to be, "Because the urban bank robber cannot easily predict when a satisfactory parking opportunity will occur." Although this response may explain the temporal irregularities of urban bank robberies, the theoretical significance of the statement is not obvious. Throughout this study, I will describe behavioral regularities and indicate what appear to be the determining factors even when the theoretical significance of the relationship is not obvious. The specification of variables and analytic units is only one step, yet an important one, in the development of theory.

45. R. Brown, *Explanation in Social Science* (London: Routledge & Kegan Paul Ltd., 1969), p. 24.
46. Ibid., p. 23.

2

PERSPECTIVES ON CRIMINALITY

A. INTRODUCTION

Before beginning an examination of the behavioral dimensions of criminal skills, it will be helpful to locate these skills within the conceptual framework used by criminals. If we can identify the categories used by criminals in the organization of crime, crime itself will become more intelligible. When we can recognize the criminals' perspective, we will not so readily impose conventional and possibly misleading categories on the behavior under study. For example, to what extent do noncriminals and criminals share common definitions of such concepts as "job," "trade," "career," "occupation," "work," "play," "professional," and "amateur"? Does the layman's use of the term "criminal career" show that he sees similarities between illegitimate and legitimate career patterns, or does the term simply imply persistence in wrong-doing? By comparing lay and criminal perspectives on crime we shall question the validity of applying conventional occupational terminology to criminality. Furthermore, we will need to differentiate between the moral and technical dimensions of crime-related conceptual categories.

The perspectives of the layman, the criminal, and the law enforcement–corrections personnel, need to be compared. Each perspective may either confirm or call into question the utility of any other perspective.

The reconstruction of subjective perspectives is methodologically precarious, since the perspectives themselves are easily distorted by initial data selection and the later imposition of the researcher's own perspectives upon the data. For example, if one wished to discover "professionalism" in criminal behavior, numerous examples could be found. Prior notions, such as professional-amateur distinctions, may be imposed upon the data at the cost of missing more meaningful distinctions. The resulting model may be a conception of the criminal that is held neither by criminals nor by those who work most closely with them.

Depending on his purpose, the observer may, of course, organize what he sees into whatever categories he wishes, provided he distinguishes between the order he imposes upon the data and the order constituting the subjective perspective of his subjects. The problem is difficult for the ethnographer:

> Instead of dealing with documents and artifacts, the ethnographer is faced with the task of making intelligible his observations or his field notes. We have tended to think of the ethnographer as *reconstructing* the subjective standpoint of the people whose actions he observes, but we can just as easily think of him as *postulating* that standpoint in order to explain what he observes.[1]

The reader will be provided with numerous quotations, through which he will be able to check on the researcher's analytical procedures. Later chapters, in which the objective and tangible dimensions of behavior are discussed, provide further basis on which to assess the subjective perspectives presented and their relations to behavior patterns.

B. LEGAL CRITERIA AND PENAL CLASSIFICATION

The public regulation of deviance involves developing standardized procedures and categories by which the deviant may be efficiently processed. The immediate implications of the bureaucratization of law enforcement have been documented only recently. The

1. Leon J. Goldstein, "The Phenomenological and the Naturalistic Approaches to the Social," M. Natanson, ed., *Philosophy of the Social Sciences* (New York: Random House, Inc., 1963).

need for efficiency, resulting in "normal crimes" and "bargain-justice" [2] indicate that the layman can no longer impute conventional meaning to the long-standing legal definitions.

My subjects generally agreed that the number of crimes committed far exceeds the number of convictions listed on the official FPS record.[3] "You only get caught for one out of twenty things you do —sooner or later you pull a sloppy one." (no. 7) Both the inmates and the penal officials also pointed out that not all crimes listed on an FPS record need necessarily have been committed by the offender under whose name they were recorded. In other words, I found widespread recognition of bargain-justice and learned that whenever someone had served several concurrent terms for similar offences (for example, had pleaded guilty to perhaps a dozen breaking and enterings ["B & E's"] and received two years for each, with sentences to run concurrently), the bargain-justice pattern was probably operative. Police have a direct interest in criminal technique, for reasons of crime prevention and interpretation; prison administrators, on the other hand, show little interest in criminal technique. That is, the considerations relevant to running a prison efficiently appear to have little to do with the acquired criminal skills of the inmates. Neither custodians nor officials refer to inmates in terms of criminal skills. Reference may be made to the inmate's latest offence, which culminated in his confinement, but little interest is shown in his previous illegitimate behavior. In part this suggests that the FPS record cannot be taken literally—that is, it must be interpreted, as Sudnow has indicated, before it can be used as information about the person in question.[4] Such interpretation requires an understanding of routine judicial processes.

My interest in experienced property offenders was not easily understood by penal officials. One reason would be that most inmates are property offenders; secondly, officials assume that inmates, except for the very young, are *not* first-time offenders, regardless of

2. For a discussion of the way in which specific criminal acts are redefined in such a way as to expedite trial procedure, see David Sudnow, "Normal Crimes: Sociological Features of the Penal Code," *Social Problems*, 12 (Winter 1965).
3. Finger Print Serial record—the most official transcript of a person's criminal convictions, including all charges, court dispositions, and time done by the person.
4. For example, persons known as safecrackers would not be convicted as such, since the criminal code does not use the term. They would most likely be charged with breaking and entering, a charge they would share with numerous other inmates who are not safecrackers.

their official record of convictions. They base their assumption on the general theory that a young, first-time offender, unless his offence was particularly serious, would be assigned to a provincial jail. It is also assumed that the magistrate has already done some evaluative work relative to the criminal history.

For the penal official to investigate the realities of any inmate's criminal history would be both time-consuming, and, given the present operating objectives of most prisons, unnecessary. His knowledge of law enforcement procedure provides him with the interpretive techniques that make a quick glance at an FPS record meaningful enough to accommodate administrative needs. Beyond that, he relies on the in-prison reports of the inmate's behavior, and may ask for a more detailed history and assessment from persons whose duties are essentially noncustodial, for example, classifications and treatment personnel. The treatment and temporary segregation of new "fish" (inmates just admitted) might also be regarded as a period when assessments relative to administrative considerations may be made. To the extent that prison officials recognize the FPS record at best only as an indication of criminality in general, they exhibit considerably more sophistication than those criminologists who have developed elaborate theories based on the literal accept-ance and interpretation of these records. One subject, referred to me by a parole officer with the introduction "He's only got one con-viction but a lot of experience," said:

> Well, over here they don't really know, but they'll think, "Well, you didn't do just that one—you're not gonna kid us. You see, this one was knocked off or that one was knocked off and you got pinched for it, so therefore it must have been you." And you might say, "Well, could be," and you just let them draw their own conclusions. (no. 7)

Whatever interest prison officials have in the criminal history of the inmate might well be accounted for in terms of the prison routine. Officials did distinguish between those who "have a long record" and those who don't, and those doing a "long bit" and those doing a "short bit." These considerations, plus the inmates' parole po-tential, are relevant for purposes of prison work-assignments and affect the prison as an ongoing organization. It is ironical, yet quite in keeping with Goffman's concept of the total institution, that the closer one looks at prison routine, the less important noninstitutional factors become. From the perspective of the prison official, the specifics of the criminal biography, the type of crime committed, and the criminal skills acquired by the convict are of little importance, since they affect prison routine only indirectly.

More directly relevant to the prison official are some very general inmate attributes. A look at the organizational elements of prison routine may also help to account for administrators' consistent emphasis on psychological dimensions of inmates, who are frequently assessed in terms of vague notions of IQ: "He's pretty bright," or "He's dull." With reference to my research, this appeared to be related to how deceptive the inmate was expected to be in his interaction with me. The administration expects that the inmate wants "out" as soon as is legally possible, and that the "bright" inmate will recognize that getting a parole, for example, involves putting on a good act, even though that act is not necessarily indicative of sincerity. The bright inmate may also recognize that the good act alone is not enough. This awareness is favorably assessed by the administration. For one thing, such a bright inmate is abiding by the rules of the game: "Do your own time, don't cause trouble and we'll see that you get out of here." It is this behavioral dimension that may, in fact, be most central. In this sense, the administration may contrast the bright inmate with someone defined as "disturbed," "upset," or (a frequently used phrase) "not yet settled down." This is in keeping with the administration's general concern with security and absence of trouble.

It is also in the interests of administration to make use of the intelligence and the leadership ability of inmates for administrative and custodial purposes. Such abilities are more likely to be recognized because of the inmate's reputation than because of his specific criminal skill.

The penitentiary officials, they recognize this. They recognize the class distinctions, and they operate accordingly. Now you take all the key positions in prison, they're given either to the intelligent person I was talking about—like the check-writer or somebody like that, that gets off in a storm—or they're given to characters. Now if it's handling other convicts, if it's down to where you're gonna tell another convict what to do and dictate his policies to him, they always get a character to do that. . . . It's on your record. They know that I'm a character. . . . The penitentiary knows that there's characters and

there's idiots and there's rums. And your characters will always be
running the penitentiary. They can't hire enough guards.[5]

The emphasis on institution-related factors has serious implications for the prison researcher. He may have difficulty persuading
prison administrators that the inmate, as person, is relevant to the
research. For example, when I handed the clerk a slip of paper with
an inmate's name and number on it, so that he could call the inmate to my office (a procedure we had agreed upon), he habitually
responded with, "The body or the file?"

From the perspective of the records department and classification
personnel in general, the role of "body," as opposed to "file" is
interesting. In each institution, it was inconceivable to such personnel that anyone would want to see the body and not the file.
Some, I felt, took it as a personal affront regarding the value of
their written work. The classic theory of the impersonal character
of bureaucracies takes on a curious twist here. Although the body is
indeed viewed as a number (personnel refer to inmates by number
rather than by name),[6] the file itself is personified. The comments
of others are perceived of as a more accurate reflection of the person
than the person himself. In fact, the body is perceived of as a false
image. "It" may "give you a line," "b.s. you," "give you a snow
job." In contrast, the file is trustworthy. It contains absolute legal
identity, the fingerprints. In addition, it provides us with the body's
character—an account of its values and thoughts by way of psychological tests, charts, and reports. The body's ability is also indicated
by aptitude and IQ tests. The body's photograph, evidence toward
which one is inclined to react in a more personal manner, is tucked
away in an envelope at the back of the file.

5. Bruce Jackson, "Who Goes to Prison," *The Atlantic* 217, no. 1 (January
1966): 55–56.
6. The practical reason for the routine use of numbers may be accounted for,
at least in part, in terms of ease of filing. The numbers themselves, however, do
not communicate any information other than identity. The ability to remember
numbers also appears to be a criterion of status and work experience—an occupational characteristic that prison clerks share with parts-men in machinery shops.
    My own use of numbers to identify the subjects quoted is necessary to assure
anonymity. Pseudonyms are less impersonal, but they could also be taken personally by readers who might not understand their fictional character.

C. LAY AND CRIMINAL PERSPECTIVES
IN CONTRAST

It became obvious during the course of this study, that although the term "criminal" is seldom used by those who are officially designated as criminals, they understand the conventional meaning of the term. They understand that a criminal is one who has been convicted by the courts, and that the term implies a moral dimension leading to subsequent stigmatization. Furthermore, in terms of Garfinkel's concept of degradation ceremonies,[7] the term may be used to impute a *totality*—for example, a totally depraved person—amounting to a reconstruction of biography. This is not compatible with the offender's own self-image, or with his experience with other "criminals." [8]

The conventional world itself is divided into numerous subcategories of increasing specification. Many of these categories have to do with occupation, and these in turn reflect the major ingredients of status—namely one's place within the distribution of power and privilege. Like the noncriminal, the criminal requires further specification as well, when referring to persons *within* his own category.

When the layman subdivides "criminal" into more specific categories, he is inclined to use models based on conventional experience, such as professional-amateur distinctions. In addition, he may differentiate between criminals, using such terms as thieves, robbers, or murderers, and so on. Popular literature and the daily press also use this terminology.

Our question here is to determine to what extent such conceptions and criteria are shared by the offenders, and to specify those subcategories of the category "criminal" that are used by the criminals themselves (and that may differ considerably from those imputed by the conventional society).

7. Harold Garfinkel, "Conditions of Successful Degradation Ceremonies," *The American Journal of Sociology* 61 (March 1956): 420–24.
8. Note: A review of my interview notes indicates that the term "criminal" is used more frequently near the end of my interviews. This suggests either: (a) that I imposed the term, or (b) that the subject perceived a mutual understanding of the term and could use it more comfortably.

1. Basic Distinctions

(a) *"Rounder"* (*"true criminal"*): Criminals speak of "rounders" as the "true criminals"—those who are committed to the illegitimate life style, as demonstrated in reliable and consistent behavior patterns. It is in this aspect of commitment and dedication that the criminal compares the rounder with the "square," as is illustrated by an inmate:

> (WE TALK ABOUT PRISON SOME MORE AND I ASK HIM ABOUT FRIENDSHIP
> PATTERNS, AND WHETHER HE MAKES A LOT OF FRIENDS THERE. HE SAYS:)
> No, I don't. A lot of people do. It's just the environment—I wouldn't
> let myself become involved closely like that around here. One thing
> you will find about all the inmates here—all the five hundred here—
> the true criminals in here are closer to the square-johns than the rest
> of us.
>   WELL, WHOM WOULD YOU CALL A TRUE CRIMINAL? Well, someone who's
> dedicated his life to crime.
>   AND IN WHAT WAY WOULD YOU SAY THAT HE'S LIKE A SQUARE-JOHN? (HE
> ANSWERS WITH LAUGHTER.) Well, I—in the sense that he's dedicated to
> his job. I think you'll find that they're more normal than the ones
> that just come in here for one bit and then are gone. . . . I would say
> that the true criminals are the more stable of the total population
> here. (no. 35)

Number 35 is suggesting that according to some criteria, such as dedication to a job, stability, and reliability, the true criminal or rounder is actually more like a "square-john" [9] than those who are not true criminals, for example, the "bum," who will be discussed later.

Simply to be found a "criminal" by the court does not confer rounder status—one must be known and recognized as one by other persons seriously committed to the illegitimate life style. In contrast to lay perceptions, the rounder does not place any particular significance in the single conviction or even the single jail sentence; he will refer to an inmate who is a one-time offender and otherwise committed to the legitimate life style as a "square." Neither does he assume that the *absence* of a conviction necessarily implies the absence of illegitimate activity. Some of the cynicism with which the

---

9. "Squares" or "square-johns" are terms used to refer to conventional, ordinary persons who have no known association with crime and criminals.

criminal may view the legitimate order is evident in the following quotation:

> Well, I wouldn't suggest anyone start out in crime nowadays—there's nothing in safes, nothing in banks; unless he was a real good con artist, and then he'd probably be legit' anyway, 'cause that's what they are, aren't they? (no. 15)

The following is another example of commitment similar to that of the square-john. An experienced safecracker referred to bank robbers, swindlers, and safecrackers as: ". . . the higher class in the underworld. We had a pride in what we were doing." (no. 4)

It may well be that the proverbial "honor among thieves" can best be described in terms of commitment. To abide by one's word implies a desire to remain within the rounder status. Within an occupation in which the worker has no trade union protection, and in which new recruits appear to be in good supply, compliance is essential to one's continued employment. Failure to meet such responsibilities means that he must become a bum or a loner or perhaps even a square-john. As the quotation below indicates, qualities of honesty and reliability are essential to success in crime.

> WHAT ABOUT THE TAKE—HOW DO YOU SPLIT THAT UP? Oh, it's always split right down the middle.[10]
>
> IF THERE ARE THREE FELLOWS THEN IT'S A THIRD FOR EACH ONE? Oh yeh—always—that was pretty well a standard rule among pete-men in all times. You're never worried about your end. I mean, if—if you have to get out in a hurry and one guy takes all the money out of the safe and you didn't immediately split it three ways, you never worried about your third. You'd get your third right to the penny, you know, regardless of who done it. Of course, it didn't *always* work out this way. Lots of guys that would short you out. But as a rule it was always understood that everybody. . . . (no. 14)

The true criminal applies work considerations strikingly similar to those of any "straight" employer. A bank robber indicates why he broke up a working partnership:

> WHEN DID YOU DROP THAT OTHER FELLOW? Because he had money—I don't recall—. Oh yeh, I asked—one night I phoned him and I

---

10. An equal division of money ("splitting") is common procedure, but not when the partners are addicts. In that case, "All dollars and cents are measured in [heroin] caps. If one guy uses two caps and the other one, if that's how you shoot, you don't split the money." (no. 19)

wanted him to go near ——, Quebec—there's a bank that sits way, about 35 miles from there—it's called ——, and I was sentenced—I got three years on that one. And I phoned this guy, and he was drunk. And I said, "You're not fit to work tomorrow." He wanted to come to work, you see. But I said, "You're not fit—you're drunk!" So he started to give me some shit over the phone and I said, "Fuck you!" Right on the phone, you see. "I'll see you later." (no. 28)

Another facet of commitment to illegal activities is suggested by the following comments. Number 42, a bank robber, stated that persons who are taught to rat (for example, the stoolie, or stool pigeon) inside prison will never make it on the outside. He felt that such persons reveal an inability to deal with pressures and succumb too easily. Thus, when faced with financial hardship they will also succumb and steal. As for himself, he said, "I wasn't going because I was desperate—I was going because I wanted money."

That is, the true criminal does not steal against his will (any more than the true square-john goes to his work against his will). The compulsory factor in both cases was brought out when no. 42 later remarked, "When I was down to a certain level I would go out." That is, money factors dictated the temporal routine, but the method of acquiring such money is a matter of perceived choice, both for the true criminal and for the square-john. Criminals distinguish between various factors and motivations that they believe cause crime. They know that some crimes are committed in a deliberate and rational manner, others, such as those generated by frustration, may be done impulsively. They perceive of the rounder as being more like the square than the "not-true criminal," in the sense that both act on the basis of choice rather than frustration. Indeed, as no. 17 pointed out, even when a legitimate job seems out of reach, he still has a choice between welfare and crime. He himself, expressing a curious version of middle-class mentality and work ethic, would rather choose crime than ". . . collect social welfare and be a nuisance for the rest of my life."

The "rounder" category does not necessarily include those whom the courts have designated as "habitual criminal." In response to the question, "Would you consider the habitual criminal to be a true criminal?" no. 35 replied:

> Well, these habitual criminals—well, you got to come down to the individual. It's almost impossible to put people in a class here, other than to say that they're convicts. (no. 35)

Later on, during our conversation, he referred to a specific habitual criminal as a "bum."

(*b*) *The "bum":* A bank robber suggested that the bulk of the prison population consists of another category, namely people who are neither rounders nor squares, but "bums" who do not have the dedication and stability of a true criminal: "In this place you've got only thirty thieves—the rest are misfits, nuisances." (no. 41) Number 21 stated: "A criminal is someone who plans—a lot of guys go and kick in places." Still another respondent stated:

> Well, some thieves perhaps—some people who know you, they might give you a little respect, you know. They feel you know what you're doing, and you're out there trying, at least. You know, it's more a matter of respect for yourself. You're not a *bum*, you know. There are too many people just sitting around, you know. Would-be thieves—living off some broad or something. That's not my line at all. (no. 2)

(*c*) *The "young punk":* The category of "bum" must be further distinguished from that of the "young punk" versus "older fellow" distinction. The latter is essentially an age-maturity distinction. The acknowledged criminal looks at most criminal activity on the part of younger men as the work of young punks, unless it is obvious to the acknowledged criminal that these younger men "mean business" and "know what they are doing." A single unusually successful caper on the part of these young punks may change their status. If, however, the young punk continues in unsystematic and sporadic criminal activity, he will become known as a "bum."

A "solid," thoughtful younger offender would not be referred to as a "young punk." To be referred to as an "older fellow" implies both maturity and experience in crime (for example, a semiretired or retired rounder). An older, but immature person might be called a "bum," but not a "punk."

An armed robber said that young prisoners never associate with other young prisoners:

> Younger kids get an admiration for some of the big wheels and try to be like them. Most guys who get into serious crime are like that. (no. 30)

In contrast to "those who get into serious crime," he referred to those who are "unsuccessful—they don't pull their weight either working, stealing or anything." (no. 30) This definition corresponds closely to that of the bum, and resembles Cloward and Ohlin's "double failures." [11] It is also similar to the inmates' description of prison guards as being "too lazy to work and too yellow to steal."

(d) "Alkies," "dope fiends," and "normals": Certain designations such as "alky" (alcoholic) or "dope fiend" (drug addict) have specific meaning within the criminal subcultures. Both terms imply illegal activity, usually theft, as a major life-style. These categories are also somewhat different from the "rounder," "bum," and "square-john" distinctions. Although they share the dedication that rounders and squares have in common, this dedication is directed towards a goal that in turn imposes strict constraints on the total life-style. The rigidity of this life-style can be shared and appreciated only by others similarly involved. For example, no. 31 has indicated that he usually lives with female "alkies" for "companionship." This relationship is tenuous:

> She'll live with you if you've got a drink. If not, she'll move over to someone who has; maybe later she'll come back to you. ARE THEY PROSTITUTES? Oh no, definitely not—they don't take money. There are not many alky prostitutes—most such are on dope. But I have known some alcoholic prostitutes—they're not really prostitutes—they'll turn right around and spend their money with you in a bar.[12] (no. 31)

Although regularly involved in illegal behavior, few alkies or dope fiends are accorded "rounder" status. An alcoholic stated that:

> Other criminals wouldn't have a thing to do with me for pulling a caper. (HE MENTIONED SEVERAL CAPERS THAT HE'D BEEN INVITED TO GO ON, BUT ADDED THAT THOSE WHO HAD ASKED HIM HAD NOT KNOWN HE WAS AN ALKY. HE HAD NOT PARTICIPATED BECAUSE HE HAS NEVER WANTED TO:) . . . really go into crime. In fact, I'm kinda grateful that I'm an alcoholic.[13] (HIS REASON WAS AMBIGUOUS:) I used to be pretty religious —I never enjoyed crime. (HE ADDED:) If I'd have gone into crime whole-heartedly, I'd not have half the convictions. If I'd gone into

11. R. A. Cloward and L. E. Ohlin, *Delinquency and Opportunity: A Theory of Delinquent Gangs* (New York: The Free Press, 1960), p. 184.

12. This curious definition of "prostitute" is based upon how the prostitute *spends,* rather than earns her money.

13. It may be useful to view alcoholism as a means whereby persons such as no. 31 maintain a measure of role-distance from the fuller criminal role. That is, by being an alcoholic one is prevented and excused from becoming a big-time successful criminal.

stealing for stealing's sake, I'd have been, I think, fairly successful. (no. 31)

The alcoholic lacks several "rounder" characteristics. His alcoholism decreases his reliability as a partner. In addition, he lacks commitment—he is not (as no. 31 put it) "stealing for stealing's sake."

Several safecrackers mentioned that one of their acknowledged colleagues was, in fact, also a dope-fiend, but this was referred to as unusual.

To become known as a drug-user or an alcoholic may seriously affect the status of even well-known rounders. To what extent such status is permanent and irreversible is not known. Number 11, who worked in the check business for some time, related:

> When they—the people, eventually learned that I was connected with drugs, that I was using, they gradually started to have nothing to do with me. WHY? Well, because it draws heat to them. They feel they can't depend on you, and this to me is very understandable. You know, they feel that whenever they send you on anything, you've gotta have drugs along and this adds to the risk. And if you didn't have drugs, well—what would you do? You know, you—would you finger the whole situation? You know—this kind of thing—this is understandable. They're in business. It's just bad business to have anything to do with hypes. (no. 11)

The rational basis for avoiding hypes and alkies was repeatedly underscored by my respondents' comments. They generally agreed that hypes are unreliable—"will sell their soul for a cap," and are therefore particularly vulnerable to police threats and to bribery. In contrast to the bum, young punk, or rat, the hype's unreliability is not so much a reflection on his character as upon the particular nature of his state; to be betrayed by a hype is a reflection on one's own judgement, rather than on the hype. Whatever bitterness was expressed towards hypes was of this sort. In other words, the hype is a perfectly predictable type for those who are well acquainted with the underworld—he is to be avoided as a work companion but not to be feared or mistrusted.

In contrast to alkies, hypes are widely recognized as being among the best of thieves. Their daring and highly developed skills are widely recognized. The criminal acts of the alky, on the other hand, are characterized by inept bungling. Although the hype and alky are accorded lower status for reasons of their unreliability, low status is also accorded certain other criminals, but for reasons of morality. For example:

> Rapists—no one will associate with a rapo. Why rape when there's lots of girls around? A thief takes property—that can be replaced; but a rapist—well, the girl, you can't change that. (no. 41)

Similar evaluations were made of petty thieves who used violence when robbing older and generally helpless victims.

2. Professionals and Amateurs

Although used by both laymen and academics, the category "professional criminal" was seldom used by my subjects; even well-known rounders did not refer to themselves as professionals. When I enquired about the concept they were unable to identify anyone as a professional. One must conclude, therefore, that the concept of the "professional criminal" lacks objective reference in the community under study, or that this category is synonymous with "rounder."

Since no inquiry was made of laymen, on the issue, the meaning of the layman's category "professional criminal" cannot be ascertained with any finality. It is obvious that lay categories cannot include all facets of the technical definitions of "professional," as the term is defined by academics. For example, Hughes states, "Now the conventional and evaluative term "profession" carries as connotation the contention that there is no conflict of interest or perspective between professional and client." [14] Clearly this definition cannot be applied readily to criminals! [15]

In his study, Sutherland compares the "professional thief" with the definition of the learned professions as defined by Carr-Saunders and Wilson.[16]

> The profession of theft has most of these characteristics. It has technical skill, an exclusive group, immunity from punishment which

14. Hughes, "The Sociological Study of Work: An Editorial Forward," *American Journal of Sociology,* LVII, no. 5 (March 1952): 425.

15. With the exception, perhaps, of those criminals who work with the "victim" for their mutual benefit, for example, in insurance frauds. It is not likely, however, that the layman has these persons in mind when speaking of professional criminals.

16. Excerpts from Sutherland's *The Professional Thief* are included in Howard Vollmer and Donald Mills, *Professionalization* (Englewood Cliffs, N.J.: Prentice-Hall, Inc., 1966).

almost amounts to a license from the state to steal, a degree of monopoly growing out of their exclusive group relationship and of their recognition by the agents of the state. Each of these is less formal than in other professions. They do not have written constitutions for their groups or licenses which they may hang on their office walls. They do have the informal equivalents of constitutions and licenses.

The one characteristic listed by Carr-Saunders and Wilson which they lack is the ethical standards which minimize the pecuniary motive. When this point was mentioned to this professional thief, he admitted that his profession did not have this characteristic, but he added that the medical and legal professions would have very few members if that were used as a criterion of membership.[17]

The layman probably includes several of the criteria listed by Sutherland, when using the term "professional criminal." The model probably incorporates concepts such as specialization, skill, wit, commitment to crime, membership in a criminal sub-culture—the latter providing both opportunity for practice and relative immunity from the law.

Sutherland notes that the professional thief:

. . . did not make a comparative study of professions as a method of reaching a conclusion that stealing may be a profession. Rather he assumed that it was and applied the name "profession" in accordance with the traditional language of his group.[18]

Einstadter, in his study of armed robbery, makes frequent and direct comparisons with his data and Sutherland's. He discovered little similarity between the behavior of his subjects and the behavior of Sutherland's professional thieves.

From the foregoing comparison it becomes obvious that the group of careerist robbers seems to bear only slight resemblance to the mob that Sutherland describes.[19]

Given Sutherland's data, one would be willing to conclude that the "professional"/"amateur" distinction is useful when differentiating between various categories of thieves. Its utility, however, may be questioned when applied across different criminal behavior systems. To speak of "professional thieves" and "professional armed robbers" implies a similarity unsupported by empirical data. In fact,

17. Sutherland, *The Professional Thief*, p. 216.
18. Ibid., p. 215.
19. Einstadter, "The Social Organization of Armed Robbery," p. 70.

Einstadter suggests that, given the differences between his subjects and Sutherland's, it would be more descriptive to speak of his subjects as "career robbers" rather than "professional robbers." [20]

My own data suggest that some, but not all of the characteristics associated with professionalism are incorporated in the category of "rounder." With reference to my subjects, the category "rounder" is directly related to the world as they know it, whereas "professional criminal" is conceptualized only abstractly. Since the term "amateur" is frequently used by criminals it may be useful at this point to explore its dimensions. The "amateur"/"experienced" distinction made by criminals bears some resemblance to the "amateur"/"professional" distinction the layman makes.

The "amateur"/"experienced" distinction is essentially a *skill* distinction. A job is said to have been done by "someone who knew what he was doing," rather than "by a professional." Although he may not refer to himself as a "professional," the experienced criminal does distinguish between the skilled and the inept criminal. Each type of crime has its own peculiar terminology for both the experienced and inexperienced. For example, experienced bank robbers refer derogatively to "note pushers" [21] as persons who don't know what they are doing, and do not acknowledge them as bank robbers. The experienced criminal does not want to be identified with the one-time, blundering offender, or with the alcoholic who has experience but not ability. As was stated, a person committing a crime is evaluated as "knowing what he's doing" or "not knowing what he's doing." The former elicits admiration, the second, contempt.

The terminology of the public media seldom distinguishes between such a "professional" caper and an "amateur" attempt. This is disturbing to criminals, since to be identified with "armed robbers" in general, lowers the status of the skilled operator.

IS IT TRUE THAT THE NUMBER OF BANK ROBBERIES HAS INCREASED? Well, the number of bank robberies in the sense of goin' in with a *note* has certainly increased, but an out-and-out armed robbery, when they say "bank robberies" they are including all of that, but when you take away all—all those with a note, or who are drunk— there was a drunk convicted yesterday, wasn't there? I DON'T KNOW.

20. Ibid., p. 71.
21. "Note pusher": someone (usually armed) who robs banks by handing the teller a note demanding money.

Yeh—2.5 reading! [22] I mean, 2.5—you're in bad shape! Yeh——— convicted him. He went in with a note. Here's a—there's a bank robbery, I mean, you know, on the sheet. (no. 32)

The above quotation shows the criteria by which this informant made his own distinctions. Anyone robbing a bank with a 2.5 reading had to be an amateur. He would not classify this as a bank robbery. This was simply "goin' in with a note."

> There's two types of bank robbers; there's those note-droppers. We call 'em wicket-men. It's touch and go there. If somebody says "scat," you know, they'll run and all they've got is a note. Or it might be kind of a nutty person—might shoot someone. We've got that type in here too, but they're not considered in this. . . . (no. 15)

One respondent, who had robbed a bank with others as inexperienced as himself, said:

> I'm in for bank robbery, but I'm not a bank robber. At least I'm a miserably poor one—in fact, I'm a poor criminal. (no. 6)

The amateur is not to be confused with the young punk. To be considered an "amateur" instead of a "young punk" involves the benefit of hindsight. The successful criminal may look upon his earlier bumbling activities as "amateurish." An accomplished burglar referred to his earlier activities in this way:

> That was a B & E on houses. That'd be in Vancouver. I was just a kid and I was looking for money. And I wasn't stealing anything; like some guys would walk in and take furniture and everything. But I was just young and I didn't know much. I was just going out looking for the money, you know. (no. 39)

This suggests that as a kid he could steal nothing else than money. He was not a "thief," since he had no connections with fences, whereby the theft of articles is made viable. He was restricted in what he could do—so much so that he did not qualify as a "thief." I asked:

> COULD YOU MAKE A LIVING OFF THIS KIND OF THING? Well, I guess you could if you were taking, like radios and TVs and you had a way of getting rid of them. Then I imagine you could, yeh. BUT JUST TAKING MONEY, COULD YOU MAKE A LIVING THAT WAY? No, as a kid, maybe. . . . (no. 39)

22. A standard measurement of alcohol content, taken with breath tests.

A significant distinction between the amateur and the experienced criminal has to do with orientation towards law enforcement. This has been recognized by both Sutherland [23] and Maurer,[24] although only in part. Both Sutherland and Maurer suggest that the professional is one who has developed skills and political power of the sort that minimize his chances of being convicted. My own data suggest the importance of distinguishing between detection and conviction. The amateur criminal's central concern is to avoid *detection;* the experienced criminal is concerned that he avoid *conviction.* Experienced criminals indicated a general disregard for anonymity. They didn't particularly mind if the police "knew" they had pulled a particular caper. The important factor for the experienced criminal was that "they have nothing on me." That is, there must be no evidence that will "stand up" in court. They are aware that their particular methods of operation and their technical skills and patterns do away with their anonymity, and that the police will "know" who did it. Although they will try to avoid arousing police pressure ("heat"), their central concern is that "the police have nothing on me."

> Now, that's the funniest part. Now we became really professional in our type of work, because the way we were working, the police knew that we were working, but the way we worked, they couldn't possibly bring any charge against us. For example, I'll describe you very briefly a bank robbery that we done. (no. 28)

The amateur, on the other hand, speaks in terms of "nobody knows who did it." Clinard and Quinney, when summarizing the typology developed by Reckless,[25] in 1961 (ordinary crime, organized crime and professional crime) make the following statements:

> Professional criminals, as the third type of career criminals, are highly skilled and are thus able to obtain considerable amounts of money without being detected. Because of organization and contact with other professional criminals, these offenders are able to escape conviction.[26]

Note their further distinction:

23. Sutherland, *The Professional Thief.*
24. Maurer, *The Big Con.*
25. Walter C. Reckless, *The Crime Problem,* New York: (Appleton-Century-Crofts, 1961).
26. M. Clinard and R. Quinney, *Criminal Behaviour Systems: A Typology,* New York: Holt, Rinehart and Winston Inc., 1967, p. 9.

> Ordinary criminals lack organization to avoid arrest and conviction. Organized criminals, on the other hand, through a high degree of organization are able, without being detected or convicted, to specialize in activity which can be operated as a large-scale business.[27]

Although the above indicates some awareness of the detection/ conviction distinction, the rationale for this distinction is not clear. We are told that the professional criminal is not detected because of his skill, the ordinary criminal is detected because he lacks organization, and the organized criminal escapes detection because of his organization. My own data include no one who would fit the above "professional criminal" category. My "experienced criminals" were often highly skilled, largely unconcerned with detection, and escaped conviction, not because of contacts but because they left no "evidence" in the legal sense. "Everybody knew I had done it, even the judge said so, but they had no evidence." (no. 25) The nature of both these skills and of "evidence" will be discussed in subsequent chapters.

The concept of "professional" held by my subjects is of a highly skilled person who engages in crime but has little or no social contact with rounders. The professional is viewed as one who treats crime strictly as a business rather than as a life-style. Respondents believed such persons were operating, but none knew any personally.

In contrast, a rounder is one who participates in the social activities of other rounders. To be a rounder implies the need for and receipt of social acceptance by other rounders. Rounders share not only a criminal trade and its profits, but also a commitment to a distinctive life-style.

A respondent, now fifty years old, who had been involved in crime "all my life," was asked, "Would you call yourself a professional criminal?" He replied:

> No—I don't think so, because I'm not money hungry. I'm not out to make a fortune, like some people want to make that great big one and retire. No—I'm not money-hungry, you know. I won't fight over it—let's say you're cutting a stake up, like some guys they see an extra quarter and they want to fight over it. I was never like that. I was never—I don't think I could be called a professional. You know, that's *my* viewpoint—from their viewpoint I am. You know, I hang around with the guys doin' the big time, and the guys that have done the big crimes and so on and so forth, but then, who else am I going

27. Ibid.

to hang around with? I can't talk the same langauge as some of them
people. (no. 15)

3. The Criminal as Specialist

The distinctions set forth in the Criminal Code (for example,
theft, homicide, rape) are not particularly useful to administrators
for purposes of managing a prison. Because prison administrators
often deal repeatedly with the same offender, yet with reference to
dissimilar criminal acts, they do not translate the magistrate's "guilty
of theft" into "thief." This "thief" may have been met earlier under a "guilty-of-armed-robbery" or "robber" label.

Since the layman does not keep record of the court reports he
reads of in the daily paper, he is inclined to make simple transla-
tions, such as "guilty of theft" means "thief." He may also impute
to the criminal subculture that which he is familiar with in a highly
bureaucratic society, such as high degree of division of labor and
specialization. Such perspectives are supported by complicated de-
tective stories and the conventional concept of the professional
criminal.

How valid are these concepts when applied to the behavior of
criminals? Does the concept of specialization "fit" our data describing such behavior? This question will be answered by referring to
the language and behavior of the subjects under study.

(a) "Having a line": Like members of the legitimate society, criminals may refer to themselves in specific occupational terms. The
nearest criminal linguistic equivalent to specialization is known as
"having a line." One respondent, after referring to himself as a shoplifter, added: "Everybody's got a line—I got that line." (no. 33)
Another stated:

> Such bugs are hard to beat—I would go get somebody who could
> handle them. Locks are *my* specialty, others go for bugs,[28] still others,
> cans.[29] (no. 13)

Increasing technological complexity has generated specialization
in both legitimate and criminal contexts. This is particularly true
for those crimes involving surreptitious entry. Better alarm systems,

28. Burglar alarm systems.
29. Safes.

more difficult locks, hinges, and so on, require study and experience. Such experience and specialization is, as in the square world, a saleable quality.

> On numerous occasions I've been approached just for that reason—guys are having trouble gettin' an "in." (no. 13)

Another example:

> So we drove to that small town, and by the way, all the banks that I done was mostly out of the city. And contrary to ———, he's a specialist to work in the city, you know, at Montreal. And I'm the type of guy that works outside the city. (no. 28)

In a later chapter we will discuss some of the factors that encourage or discourage specialization, and the criteria by which various lines are evaluated as career possibilities.

Although most subjects interviewed felt they "had a line," this should not be understood as a restrictive factor in any "legal" or organized fashion. That is, the criminal is not troubled by trade union or professional legislation restricting the behavior of its members. He is hampered in some cases by technical and associational factors, as we shall see later in our discussion of the technical aspects of crime. His peers do not expect him to stay only in his line—the shoplifter may do a B & E on occasion, and the bank robber, a burglary.

One inmate whose line was hotel-prowling, stated that there was probably no crime he hadn't committed at one time or another. He pointed out that the bank roll determines what type of crime will be engaged in:

> If you've got big money you can do a con job—impress someone. If you're broke, you've got to go on the boost. (no. 12)

Even within the line of hotel-prowling, economics may determine how such work is done. Number 12 pointed out that in the better hotels the locks cannot be loided,[30] nor can they be easily picked without arousing suspicion. If the burglar has money, he can get a master key made—this is done by first checking into the hotel as a legitimate customer. The burglar uses the lock from his own room,

---

30. "Loiding" a door involves the insertion of a sturdy yet flexible piece of plastic between the door and its frame in such a way that the latch is pushed back.

either removing it entirely and substituting another, or removing all but one pin (leaving just enough to keep the lock working). He added, "I can't make a master key, but for a price you can get some-one who can." (no. 12) That is, certain persons are able and willing, for a fee, to make a master key from the door lock itself. If the bur-glar cannot afford this, but wishes to remain in hotel work, he can "run openers," that is, work the cheaper hotels where the locks are easier.

It is acknowledged that there is a temptation, following a big score, to "live off it" till it is gone. However, the penalty for such behavior is that one must then go back to less profitable and prob-ably more dangerous types of crimes. Good money management is as important to the criminal as to the civilian. It is difficult in the first place for an addict to gain enough capital to stay off the "boost" (shoplifting), but an addict with money can afford to use safer work techniques and can live much more cheaply by buying his drugs in larger quantity.

A variation from one's line may also be brought about by new opportunities, particularly when one's regular line does not appear to be viable at the time.

> And since I didn't have anything going at the time, I decided to go in on it. So when I was approached on this thing, I didn't have any-thing going at the time and they said, "We want you to go to such and such a state." They explained the whole scam to me and they said there had been a trial run made on this. (no. 11)

Strict specialization may be both impractical and impossible:

> When you're stealin' you don't just steal with one fella'—you fill in with anybody who finds out something. You begin to get the idea? Stealing for a living isn't just being a burglar or stick-up man. You've got to be able to take advantage of them regardless of what the condi-tions are. A lot of people think once a stick-up man, always a stick-up man. Well, you can't run around stickin' up people every day of the week like a workin' man. Maybe something worth sticking up only shows up every two or three months. In the meantime you're doing this and that, changing around, doing practically anything to make a dollar.[31]

Although criminals are likely to limit their activities to styles with which they are familiar, work outside their line may be ac-

31. Sutherland, *The Professional Thief*, p. 80.

cepted if it is recommended to them by someone who is trustworthy:

YOU SAY YOU WERE NOT JUST CONFINED TO DOING SAFES? Oh no. Actually you'd do anything that you figure was a good score—you figured you could make it, regardless of what it was. All the time you get different guys comin' to you and saying—"I got a good score!," "I got this." And some might be safes and some might not be, but you know these might come from guys that aren't pete-men.[32] But if they've got a good name and you know they're alright, you may go along with what they've got. (no. 14)

I asked no. 14 whether a pete-man would do B & E's without looking for a safe:

Well, yes. Depending on what it was, you know. If it was worth your while—if there's money in it, sure you would. (HE WOULD NOT, HOWEVER, PICK UP STUFF THAT WAS HARD TO TURN INTO CASH.) (no. 14)

The safecracker quoted below suggests that specialization is based on personal work preference rather than specialized skills. Implied also is recognition of the danger of engaging in types of crime with which one is unfamiliar:

WOULD A PETE-MAN HAVE THE SKILLS TO DO, LET'S SAY, A BANK ROBBERY? Oh yeh, but few pete-men would go on a bank robbery—you got—one reason being most of them dislike very much to use a gun. If you're goin' on a bank robbery you got to go there with a gun and you've got to be prepared to use it, because if you don't you're crazy. Because you'll get your head blown off yourself if you don't. You're usin' a gun which gets you more time—you may end up shootin' somebody or gettin' shot yourself, whereas breaking and entering is surreptitious entry—see what I mean—nobody's supposed to see you, see? (no. 14)

"Having a line," therefore, implies a generalized work preference and a related repertoire of skills, which can be adapted to various related crimes should reasons of practicality, economics, and unique opportunities so dictate. To diverge from one's line, however, invokes the hazards implicit in lack of practice and unfamiliarity. Only in unusual circumstances will someone known as "having a line" engage in crimes to which his skills are ill-suited and for which he has a personal distaste. Nor does the criminal line necessarily in-

---

32. The term "pete-man" refers to "safecracker." Although the two terms are sometimes used synonymously, in its more precise meaning, "pete-man" refers only to those safecrackers who use explosives.

volve a progressive movement from the general to the specific, as is the case in conventional career patterns. The line is simply indicative of some consistency in one's choice of illegal activity.

(b) *Variations within a line:* One's line does not necessarily indicate status ranking. That is, one can be a good or a poor B & E man. As stated, criminals are neither restricted nor protected by union or professional codes; there are no recognized standards that officially designate anyone as a "B & E man." The standards that do exist are informal and have to do with the quality of one's performance within a specific line.

Good and poor performance within a line may or may not be accorded a more specific designation. The poor thief is a "petty thief." The poor B & E man does "kick-ins." These criteria, more so than one's line, indicate status. The good thief may occasionally engage in petty theft, and some B & E's may turn out to be nothing more than kick-ins. But if the exceptions become the rule, one's status may change. An experienced burglar provided the following commentary:

> AND YOU WERE NOT ENGAGED IN PETTY THEFT? Oh, a lot of thefts were pretty petty—they weren't intended to be that way. Don't misunderstand me—I'm not trying to make out that I'm a high powered thief or anything. A lot of stuff I did panned out to be ham sandwich stuff. Oh yeh—I've done my share of petty-ass kick-ins—like medical dental buildings and drug-stores, just to get drugs, you know. And a lot of times I've been broke. (no. 2)

A shoplifter distinguished between his own skills and the efforts of "rubby-dubs" (alcoholics) by saying: "All these rubby-dubs lift socks. Socks is nothing—like a balloon. I take a few pair, but socks is nothing. (no. 3)

A further distinction is made in terms of one's position within a given "line" or specialty. We have already indicated that persons may be ranked in terms of standards of performance. Distinctions having to do with the *scale* of one's illegal operations, as well as distinctions essentially similar to employer-employee relationships are made. Number 16 referred to himself as a "small fry," pointing out that "big shots" have men like himself who work for them. He did not associate the "big shots" with any particular type of "line," but described them as the "smart guys . . . who sit back and let the others do the work." (no. 16)

4. The Criminal as Prisoner

Judging from the professional literature, one is led to believe that incarcerated persons represent the inept, criminal washouts, and as such are not representative of criminals in general. It is also probable that the layman views prisoners as being "less successful" criminals. My own data indicate that such generalizations must be qualified by recognizing the varieties of crime and its technical dimensions.

> The law of averages is against you—I don't care how good you are —you'll end up in jail at some time. (no. 44)
> DID YOU EVER KNOW ANY SAFECRACKERS WHO NEVER DID ANY TIME? No—I can't say I did. DO YOU THINK THERE WERE SUCH? That's a hard thing to say, you know—if there were such, I wouldn't know about them because if they never got caught, how would you know? But any of the ones I ever knew, they all done time at one time or another. (no. 14)

When asked what would characterize a "best safecracker," no. 14 begins by saying that it's experience that matters:

> I used to go out two and three times a week and through that I gained a fair bit of experience, but I'd say—I don't know how anyone would say so and so's the best—but I don't think there is any such thing as bein' the best. There's some guys that are smarter than others, that's all—more cagier and more efficient and—an naturally the more safes you blow the more you know about it, you see. And like I say, this was one thing I lacked, because I did too much time to get the experience.
> DOING A LOT OF TIME—IS THAT A SIGN OF NOT BEING AT THE TOP OF THE LADDER IN THE SAFECRACKING SKILLS? No, no—I wouldn't say that. I would say that some of the real good safecrackers did an awful lot of time—some of the best did a lot of time. But I would think it's just due to a person's own fault, or maybe carelessness. It's got to be that. Or maybe too much activity, which I think was my case. I used to go out a lot more than I had to, and you know—real often. And ———— used to say—the more times you go out the more chance you have of gettin' caught, you see. (no. 14)

In the following chapter, I argue that safecracking expertise is maintained only by frequent practice. The quotation just given shows that frequent practice also increases the probability of being

apprehended. In other words, expertise and frequency of conviction may be directly, rather than inversely, related. Statements as
to the relationship between expertise and prison experience must
take into account the distinctions between various forms of crime.

The prison sentence provides networks of social relationships
that the exconvict may either nourish or discard. The rounder is
one who maintains such association and is identified by the subculture as a member. This involves continued support of rounder
norms, and, more or less, participation in illegal activities and in
rounder social activities. In Western City, several hotels are referred
to by criminals as "rounder hotels." The distinction between the
rounder and others consists not only of interaction, but also of the
places of such interaction.

(a) *How much time done, and where:* One of the factors by which
a rounder may be identified is the amount of time he has spent in
prison. To a rounder, this indicates the degree of criminal involvement. The amount of time may consist of a series of shorter "bits,"
or a single "long bit" (also known as "big time").

The significance of the prison experience bears a striking resemblance to that of the college or university experience. Both provide
formal criteria for position and status. Both provide networks of
association. The nature of the academic association is further speci-
fied when the academic specifies which institution he attended. In
a similar way, the location of the prison experience is also an important item of information. Prisons are known to rounders in
terms of the network of social relationships surrounding them.
Thus, the Prairie Penitentiary was known for years as a place where
safecrackers might be found. To have done time there was to say
that one was acquainted with certain rounders. Inmates at the
Western Penitentiary, who are doing time for armed robbery in the
East, are ascribed high rounder status, since inmates "know" it is
the policy of the Penitentiaries Commission to transfer convicted
Eastern bank robbers who have worked in gangs to Western prisons.

Furthermore, the distinction between a jail and a penitentiary
experience is crucial. Full membership in the rounder community
involves a graduation from jail to penitentiary sentences.

(b) *Prison subculture and "doing your own time":* Academic and
journalistic literature make much of what is referred to as "inmate

subculture." The image of the "criminal as prisoner," which is communicated to the reader, tends to focus on matters of prisoner stratification systems and on prisoner ideology.

The nature of the prison subculture, as well as its relationship with the "outside," may be partly clarified by examining the notion of "doing your own time." This expression is frequently used by inmates and has several implications. First of all, doing your own time is an indication of adaptation to a total institution. That is, the outside is deliberately made irrelevant. Inmates agreed that the best way to "do time" is to forget about the outside, though they did not all consider themselves equally successful in achieving this. Persons doing big time agreed that all outside social ties must be severed. This does not imply permanence, but rather a moratorium. The inmate who does his own time, doesn't care about politics, the war in Vietnam, or anything outside. He probably knows about what is going on, but deliberately develops an attitude of no concern. When I asked, "Why?," I received a rather standard and highly rational reply: "What difference would it make?—I can't do anything about it here."

> What's the use? You're in jail; what the hell's the use of writin' to somebody outside? It don't do any good. The less contacts you have with the outside when you're inside, the easier your time is.[33]

Nor does there appear to be much room for idealism in terms of changing the prison structure or of putting pressure on the administration. Frequent references were made to "the riot" as an example of how open resistance to the administration results in even greater restriction. The inmate who is trying to arouse militancy among his fellow inmates is viewed as one who has not yet learned to do his own time.

A second dimension of "doing your own time" involves inmate-inmate relationships. It is generally acknowledged that being sentenced to the penitentiary involves serious deprivation, and frequently social tragedy. Inmates are aware that some of them are constantly in danger of "cracking up" under the strain. I inquired as to the amount of inmate social support given to those who couldn't bear up under the pressures: "How do inmates help and

33. J. B. Martin, *My Life in Crime*, New York: Signet Books (1952), p. 135.

support each other?" I was surprised to find strong agreement to the effect that such social support is largely absent and in fact, deliberately avoided: "You've got to learn to do your own time," or "You can't cry on anyone's shoulder."

> If you're in a dorm with forty guys—a guy gets a letter from home that someone died. Well, he's cryin' on your shoulder and makin' you do the hard time; or maybe he goes berserk in the night and stabs some guys. When I'm alone I can relax,[34] otherwise I'm very high-strung. (no. 9)

Two reasons were given to account for this apparent lack of compassion. Inmates feel they have nothing to offer—they can change neither the internal (prison) nor external (outside) problems that the inmate faces. In addition, one must avoid hoping for favorable changes in one's condition, and avoid arousing what are likely to be false hopes in others. Secondly, each inmate is probably bearing all the problems he is personally capable of handling. "I can't worry about his wife too!" Despite its generally asocial character, doing your own time does not preclude maintaining primary relationships, though these are usually limited to two or three friends per inmate.

Although doing your own time may well be viewed as a functional adaptation to prison, I am suggesting that the implications of doing your own time militate against the full development of what is usually included in the concept of "subculture." In doing his own time the inmate is able to meet the demands of prison routine without relinquishing the norms and status distinctions meaningful to him outside the prison. This perspective incorporates both the position of the functionalists and of those, like Irwin and Cressey,[35] who see the prison culture as an extension of the "outside" criminal values and behavior systems.

34. For reasons such as these, inmates are not entirely happy with the group emphasis incorporated into some contemporary prison architecture for rehabilitative reasons. Inmates also believe that building more comfortable prisons will result in judges handing down more prison sentences, and for longer periods of time.

35. John Irwin and Donald Cressey, "Thieves, Convicts, and the Inmate Culture," *Social Problems,* 10, no. 2 (Fall 1962).

E. RECOGNITION AND REPUTATION

The everyday legitimate world includes a variety of public *rites de passage* by which the public ratifies the right of a certain individual to assume a certain role. This may include the right to use certain public symbols (such as the wedding ring), or it may consist of a private document or license that can be produced if necessary. On the other hand, some persons (for example, leaders) may be acknowledged informally, without formal ratification of that role.

These matters, complicated enough in the legitimate society, are even more complex when applied to criminals. The criminal is a part of at least three worlds or defining communities—namely, his fellow criminals, square-johns, and law enforcement personnel, particularly the police. He recognizes the evaluations of each as important, even though they may differ radically from each other.

For most citizens the courts provide a highly useful simplification process. Certain officials are assigned the task of differentiating between the criminal and noncriminal (just as psychiatrists do with reference to mental health). The ritual associated with court processes adds the stamp of legitimacy and validity to the decisions made. The difficulties the exconvict has in being socially accepted indicate the irreversible character of such a definition. This suggests that the lay person who defines criminals as "those convicted by the courts" is unlikely to reverse this definition; he also prefers to believe that persons not so convicted are not criminals.

1. On Being "Known"

As numerous studies indicate, policemen are not as readily impressed by the decisions of the courts as are lay people. They "know" before such decisions are made who is guilty or innocent, and are not likely to change their opinion as a result of the court decision.[36]

The lay person may be content to distinguish between a criminal and a noncriminal, but the police are interested in more specific subcategories. Some of these might correspond to those already discussed as relevant categories used by criminals themselves, but since policemen were not interviewed, this must be left to speculation. It does

36. This is documented in Skolnick, *Justice Without Trial.*

seem reasonable to suppose that police are interested in imputing some degree of consistency and predictability to the criminals they encounter so that they can be more easily recognized as having done a particular "job." This is seen by the criminals:

> Once you are known as one who does B & E's the police can pick you up and charge you with anything[37] on the slate. (no. 33)

This suggests the establishment of a line by a criminal is useful to the police, but involves a danger for the criminal in terms of unwanted recognition. This avenue of recognition is also useful to those business institutions most vulnerable as victims of criminal activities, for it is in their interest to be able to differentiate between legitimate and illegitimate customers. For example, no. 33 doesn't seem very choosy as to where he would boost. When he mentions the Bay, I ask whether the clerks at the Bay would recognize him, since I heard they studied pictures of known shoplifters:

> I'm not known as a shoplifter. The Bay knows the shoplifters. WHAT ARE YOU KNOWN AS? Just an ordinary drunken thief, that's all. (no. 33)

Because he is not "known" as a shoplifter, he will not be suspected as one.

To become known as a specialist invokes the danger of police recognition and suspicion; on the other hand, we have noted that criminal specialization is not particularly restrictive. That is, one may leave one's line occasionally to do different jobs. None of my respondents indicated that such movement was consciously designed to frustrate police, though one may reasonably deduce that this is one of the consequences.[38]

As a criterion of status it is not as important to be known for any particular line, as it is to be known as someone who has a line. To be known implies recognition of rounder qualities; it does not seem to matter much what one's particular line is. One qualification should be added—the young kids, or punks, appear to pay more attention to the specific line itself than do the older fellows. It may be that they carry over to the criminal world some of the square cri-

37. The context of this statement implies that the "anything" refers to any type of B & E, rather than any type of crime.
38. It would be useful to determine how rigid the policeman's "typing" proves to be. That is, having typed someone as a B & E man, is such a person ruled out as a potential booster?

teria for assigning status. They are not yet socialized to the new value system.

Also important is the matter of reputation. If to be known is more important than to be known *as a pete-man,* then to be known as a *good* pete-man is more important than to be known as a pete-man. The level of performance within one's line forms the basis for the criminal's reputation. My respondents appeared to assign equal status to the good B & E man and the good safecracker. Expertise is more admired than the form of its application.

> I know of two particular fellows that were very good safecrackers —they were very good. I've worked with them and done time with them and everything else. But I know these two in particular have gone in for hotel thefts, like room-prowling, I guess you would call it. And it really pays off—big money. (no. 14)

2. How One Becomes Known

As indicated earlier, there are some obvious reasons why it is hazardous to become known; it was generally assumed that if one is known to one's peers, one is also known to the police. All my respondents took for granted that there was a steady flow of information from the larger criminal culture to the police agencies. Information that was not to get to the police had to be kept from this culture as well—and, conversely, it is possible to communicate with the police via this culture. An apartment burglar stated:

> Nobody in this area knew what I was doing—I wouldn't, as I said before, flash around a roll, because I never hung around with anybody. You see, this is the trouble with most people in here (prison)—they all drink at the same place. So you walk into there—let's say it's a bar or a pub or something. So you walk into there, and you sit down and these people all sitting around, and you can tell who is making out all right and who isn't. By who is flashing the roll around and who is buying the rounds, and stuff like this. Well, I never hang around with the criminal element when I'm on the street and all. For instance, if I hire a partner who goes on scores with me from time to time, then I wouldn't hang with him. (no. 35)

The above person would not become known until he does time. If the trial indicates a consistency in his history of crime, this reputation will be ascribed to him by other inmates. From then on he is known.

Criminals, particularly those who are known, seek their social rewards within the criminal element. As one known safecracker put it, "What's the point of scoring if nobody knows about it?" (no. 32) In his case, he tended to celebrate a good "score" [39] by buying the drinks for everyone. Others are more subtle, but manage some social recognition as well:

> Well, actually that's kinda hard to answer because when you rob banks you don't actually—I don't come around telling you—I don't tell the guy next door. I didn't tell this guy. I didn't tell anybody, because it was none of their business. But little by little people around town know that "this guy—he don't work; man, he's doin' somethin'!" You see what I mean—it's just supposition. You hear it somewhere along the line, somewhere along the grapevine—they think, but they don't know, you see. (no. 7)

Further:

> SO YOU CAN'T REALLY ENJOY YOUR STATUS? No, you can't. The only part you can enjoy is when you pick up the paper and you read that such and such a gunman tore off such and such a bank. That's all you get out of it, see? [40] But then again, in a place like this here, you're right at the top.
> HOW DO ANY OF THE OTHER GUYS IN HERE KNOW THAT YOU EVER DID ANY BANKS BESIDES THE LAST ONE THAT YOU WERE CAUGHT ON? Oh, they don't know. But when you organize that like that, they know darn well that you just haven't done one—you've probably done several more before that. (no. 7)

It should not be assumed, however, that the criminal's display before his peers is entirely a matter of seeking status, or that it constitutes a weakness on the part of the criminal. Instead, it is more useful to view it as a "demand characteristic" of the criminal's trade; a display in the sense that the term is used by Turner, who points out that "work is not merely done, but oriented to as a display," and that each occupational setting is oriented in part to "particularly significant audiences" which must be taken into account by the worker.[41] For the criminal, one such significant audi-

---

39. A successful property offence. "Score" refers both to the event (also known as a "caper") and to the money or property stolen.
40. This suggests an unacknowledged consequence of newspaper reporting. For example, for some criminals it provides the only source of social recognition.
41. Roy Turner, "Occupational Routines: Some Demand Characteristics of

ence is his peer group of fellow criminals. He relies on them for vital information that determines the course of his daily activities—which parts of the city are "hot," which fence is in need of what at any one time, and so on. Since by definition his work is secret, it is he who must communicate his successes and competence to others. (Also, by definition, failures are highly visible, being made public via numerous agencies.) Communication of competence may well be necessary for him to find or be offered continued work.

It would seem paradoxical to suggest that one of the criminals' "significant audiences" is the police and that he would think of his work as a "display" for them. By this I mean more than the fact that the criminal knows the police will see his work. It is to suggest that the criminal is sensitive to the police as an important reference group; he wants them to think highly of his workmanship as a criminal. Besides his fellow criminals, the police are the only other persons capable of evaluating and, therefore, "appreciating" criminal work skills. Such display orientation is possible if we recall our earlier "experienced"/"amateur" distinction. It was noted that the experienced criminal is concerned with lack of *evidence* rather than with secrecy. Providing that his display does not include evidence, it is possible for him to orient his work with a police audience in mind.

The burglar quoted below feels he would lose status in the opinion of the police should he miss some money in a house burglary:

> The police even. They—police will say that, like "What a sucker—he missed five-hundred dollars—how the hell'd you miss five-hundred dollars?" See? "If he took forty to fifty dollars, why didn't he take the others?" That's what they're going to say. But if you can't find it, how the hell you goin' to take it? See—that's the whole trouble. A smart crook—a smart crook, he'll look into these things, and say, "Well, he's got some stashed here, some stashed there, some stashed on the floor"—you look all over, and you clean him, and then when they come to investigate, the police say, "Well, there was a smart aleck, eh? He took everything! He knew the layout!" You got to work that layout out. (no. 16)

Becoming known is not entirely a matter of choice. The police have developed a system of clues that indicate to them the probability of criminal involvement, as will be illustrated by the following

Police Work," (unpublished paper presented to the Canadian Sociology and Anthropology Association, June 1969), pp. 6 and 7.

account. When no. 35 was seventeen years of age he frequently travelled with a friend who delivered food for a Chinese restaurant. The police stopped them one night, and successfully charged them with possession of house-breaking instruments. These "instruments" consisted of a tire iron, a pair of pliers, and a screwdriver. No. 35 claimed they were innocent at the time but, acknowledged that the police had reason to be suspicious: "In their eyes I was well-heeled at the time, so in their eyes I was doing something." (no. 35)

3. The Implications of Being Known

It is interesting to note that the clues used by policemen bear striking similarity to those used by criminals themselves. It has already been noted that the experienced criminal is not particularly worried about being known, as such, to the police. In contrast to the amateur, whose concern is with concealment, the experienced criminal's concern, as we have seen, is with evidence. He is satisfied when the police "have nothing on me."

In this sense also, the criminal who is known poses quite a different problem to the police than the criminal who is not known. For the latter, it is a question of "Who did it?"; for the former, the question is, "What have we got on him?":

> Criminals are inclined to talk shop all the time. (FOR THIS REASON POLICE OFTEN FIND OUT WHAT'S GOING ON, AND INMATES IN PRISON ALSO KNOW WHAT IS GOING ON.) When a bank's been done, we know pretty soon who done it. The police, they know half the time who done it, but they can't prove it. (no. 36)

To be accorded "known criminal" status results in the redefinition of everyday events. Respondents frequently spoke of "bum beefs," "phony beefs," "bum raps," and so on. Such beefs were defined as "a traffic beef or something." That is, a phony beef may be a legitimate charge, which is, however, made for other than the stated reasons. Both the police officer and the criminal understand the act as being symbolic. To the criminal it is a "sneaky way" for the police to apprehend someone, and such behavior is not considered entirely fair by the criminal, although he must play along with the game.

A phony beef is to be distinguished from what is referred to as "not getting a fair shake." The latter is perceived of as lack of justice, discrimination, and a violation of the rules of the game. Criminals have strong notions as to what constitutes a just sentence, and also what constitutes valid evidence. Although I have little evidence to this effect, there is reason to believe that to be known as a criminal may, in the courtroom, be beneficial rather than detrimental to the accused. That is, it is known by both prosecutor and magistrate that the accused is not ignorant of precedent, and has a fairly accurate notion of what sentence the bench may reasonably impose.

On the other hand, a criminal's reputation may effect a legal redefinition of his behavior. The example below indicates how the act of B & E may be reinterpreted by the judge in a way that would be consistent with the criminal's reputation—in this case, as an act leading toward an intended safecracking. The criminal is aware that his reputation places additional meaning on his behavior:

WHAT HAPPENED AFTER THESE TWO YEARS OF SAFEBLOWING? Went to the pen. Got caught and went to the pen. HOW DID YOU GET CAUGHT? Uh—let's see—it was during—I was going in to blow a safe and I ran into a burglar alarm, just before I started getting into burglar alarms. I ran into a burglar alarm, and naturally, before I got out of there, they were there and they pinched me and they charged me with B & E. This is all they can charge me with, in a spot like this, 'cause I've already got rid of the—as soon as I saw them coming I got rid of the fuses one way—I poured the nitro glycerine down the sink. They don't know what I had, or, you know—so they charge me with B & E and I got three years for that. As much as they suspect—like I told you, they've got to have evidence, definite evidence.

NOW, WHEN THE POLICE KNOW THAT YOU ARE OBVIOUSLY GOING TO BLOW A CAN, AS THEY WOULD HAVE IN THAT CASE—DOES THE JUDGE ALSO KNOW THAT? Officially he doesn't, but he—the prosecutor usually gets to him and talks to him. NOW, IN FACT THEN YOU ARE SENTENCED AS IF YOU WERE GOING TO BLOW A CAN? Oh yes, sure. It isn't what you did, it's what you know. Another man could come along right behind you and get charged with B & E and get six months where I get three years—for the very fact that I was a known—that I was involved in this.

WOULD YOU HAVE GOT MORE TIME IF THEY HAD FOUND ALL THE STUFF ON YOU? Oh yes, oh yes. You see, they've got an excuse now, to give you more time. You see, certain sections of the code call for—ah—breaking and entering calls for, I forget—six months to five to ten years. FOURTEEN YEARS? Yeh—it's fourteen now, but at that time it was either six to five years. Six months to five years. Explosives, carrying explosives was considered a more serious crime in their eyes, you know. (no. 29)

Being known may also provide immunity from some types of police informers. One of the interesting factors in the career of a thief is the role of the fence, particularly when the fence is also a bootlegger. There is evidence to suggest that bootleggers need police protection in order to operate—they also depend on the illegitimate order for a mandate. With reference to this, a respondent suggested that the bootlegger acts as an informer for the police, but informs only on those thieves who have no status in the criminal subculture. (no. 18)

3

SURREPTITIOUS CRIMES

The Technical Dimensions of Burglary, with Special Attention to Safecracking

A. INTRODUCTION

My data suggest that there are, essentially, three classes of criminal skills, namely: mechanical skills (involving tools and procedures), organizational skills (involving group leadership and the planning and execution of the event), and social skills (involving the management of victims and the control of tension). I am not including here those social skills necessary for participation in the criminal group.

The distinction between mechanical and social skills permits two further classifications of crime: surreptitious crime, which avoids direct confrontation with the victim (as in various forms of burglary), and overt crime, in which victim confrontation is anticipated and generally unavoidable (as in robbery). The former is characterized by the need for mechanical skills, the latter by the high degree of interpersonal skill necessary for the management of the victim. They are not differentiated on the basis of organizational skills, which depend on the nature of the particular crime being committed.

The distinction between surreptitious and overt crime is seldom made explicit by criminals, although the difference can be inferred easily if we attend to the dominant concerns expressed by them. It is inherent in the distinction between noisy and quiet work expressed below:

YOU SAID SOMETHING ABOUT WORKING WHERE IT'S NOISY AND WHERE IT'S QUIET? Well, there's a lot of people like noise—action. They want action. They go into a firm—they'll probably go there in the daytime and they go in there and they'll have a ball. They get a kick out of that—they do it in public. I like a place where it's empty, there's no noise. There's nobody in there, nobody to molest, or anything like that. And take it and leave quietly, and that's it. (no. 16)

The distinction between surreptitious and overt crimes is not the same as distinction between crimes with and crimes without victims.[1] We are not here denying the fact of victimization; the point at issue is, primarily, the presence of a victim at the scene of the crime. Further, the term "victim" must be given a wider interpretation, since a man robbed of his wallet at gunpoint is obviously a victim of a different order than a bank teller.[2]

Secondly, the importance of social skills has been acknowledged earlier by both Maurer[3] and Sutherland.[4] It is widely recognized that some types of crime, notably confidence games, involve highly refined abilities to manipulate people, predict their reactions, and so on. My own data suggest that the importance of such abilities is somewhat underrated with respect to crimes such as robbery. Carrying a gun as a persuasive device does not appear to minimize the need of manipulative skills—in fact, in order *not* to have to use the gun the robber is dependent upon just such skills.

In order to contrast crimes without victim confrontation and crimes with victim confrontation, I will describe burglary in this chapter and robbery in the next. The necessary requisite skills, be they mechanical, organizational, or social, will be indicated in each case.

The skills necessary to surreptitious crime revolve around three

1. Edwin Schur, *Crimes Without Victims* (Englewood Cliffs, N.J.: Prentice-Hall, Inc., 1965).
2. This distinction is also made by robbers, primarily in terms of possible danger to themselves.
3. Maurer, *Whiz Mob.*
4. Sutherland, *The Professional Thief.*

procedures, namely "casing," "making the in," and the act of theft itself. By "casing" I refer to the process of looking for, and assessing a potential job. This procedure will be dealt with separately in a later chapter. "Making the in" is the process of gaining entry to the place where the desired property is located and includes skills having to do with locks, burglar-alarm systems, and avoiding detection. The act of theft itself obviously refers to property acquisition. This may require opening safes, tampering with furniture, and the physical transportation of merchandise.

The burglar who wishes to enter a commercial establishment or private dwelling may be interested in cash, goods, or both. If he is interested in goods, he faces the problem of transportation and of converting the goods into cash. His technical problems, however, are largely over once a successful entry has been made. The burglar who goes for cash must be able to make a second "in"; that is, he must be able to get at the cash—a task much more problematic than that of getting at goods. He does not, however, face the problems of transportation or of being in possession of stolen goods, and of course, his take is "liquid" in economic terms.

Given these aspects, it is understandable why burglars tend to go *either* for cash, or for merchandise. It is technically difficult to come equipped both to obtain cash and to transport merchandise. The combined operation is dangerously time-consuming; further, the cash burglar may see little need to take merchandise. As one of them put it, "Why should I? If I want something, I can come back next day and buy it."

The discussion in this chapter will focus on the cash burglar, for several reasons. First of all, cash burglary illustrates the divergent skills used in what amounts to situations of double entry; secondly, it facilitates comparison with the armed robber who also is interested in cash only.[5]

Since several specific burglary techniques will be described, it should be emphasized that the list is not intended to be exhaustive. The examples are used to illustrate what are considered to be the basic principles governing the act of burglary. A burglar may be familiar with few or many specific techniques, but to be successful he must understand the basic principles, and knowing these, he must

---

5. This is in no way to underrate the sociological significance of the interaction between the merchandise burglar and the fence, and between the fence and the purchaser of stolen goods.

be able to apply them in specific ways to concrete situations. This application may call for considerable ingenuity and creativity.

B. "MAKING THE IN"

Obviously, a burglar's method of entry is significantly different from a robber's. In fact, some forms of robbery do not involve entry into a building at all (for example, on-the-street stick-ups). Other methods of entry, such as in bank robbery, are accomplished with relative ease, since the doors are usually unlocked and frequently even left open for the convenience of customers, thus serving as the natural points of entry for the robber. Unlike the burglar, the robber is much more concerned with getting out than with getting in, and his conception of "out" is probably more like "getting out of this general area" than it is with getting out of the building itself.

The burglar, on the other hand, operates at a time when neither he nor legitimate customers are welcome, and meets with closed doors. He does not face his victim, but instead the mechanical devices that indicate he is not wanted and, by their degree of complexity, the relative importance of his being kept out.

Just as the mechanical devices designed to thwart burglars vary in complexity, the entry procedures of burglars also vary from the simple and crude to the highly sophisticated and skilled. The procedure to be used depends primarily on the nature of the obstacles confronting the burglar, although factors such as his abilities, time, and need for silence may also influence the choice.

Burglars make a basic distinction between places that are "bugged" (with alarm systems) and those that are not bugged. It is assumed that domestic residences are not bugged. Procedures may vary from slitting a screen, breaking or prying open a window, to picking the door lock. Where noise is not a concern the burglar may do a "kick-in." This literally refers to a sharp kick at the spot on the door just next to the latch. Burglars assert that most doors of both houses and business establishments are so poorly made that a kick-in will usually spring the door open. The term, however, has a wider connotation and is commonly used by thieves to differentiate between a simple and a more complex "in."

House and hotel burglars are not faced with the problem of alarm systems, nor with particularly difficult locking mechanisms; but, although the actual entry for such a burglar is less problematic than for the burglar who works commercial establishments, there is the possibility that someone is present within. Furthermore, he is unlikely to find large amounts of money.

The burglar who works commercial establishments faces more difficult entry problems but believes that the probability of greater financial gain compensates for this. He may use any or all of the methods of the house burglar, depending on their adequacy. He is familiar with kick-ins, as well as other techniques that exploit structural weaknesses of buildings. He is not as likely to employ methods that involve tampering with or picking the lock, since businesses tend to have locks that are more "burglar-proof" than do houses. The commercial burglar is, however, frequently constrained by electronic alarm systems, particularly where large amounts of money are kept, as in banking establishments.

Burglars distinguish between two types of alarms—the silent alarm or bug, and those that are not silent. The silent bug is linked by telephone wires to a central detection agency. When the bug is set off, a light flashes on a panel at the agency office. The police are immediately notified and given the exact location of the burglary. The silent alarm provides the burglar with no audible or visible indication as to whether or not it has gone off.[6]

In contrast, the nonsilent bugs, when triggered, set off one or more loud gongs or bells that may be located either inside or outside the building, or both. Depending on the noise level and bell location, the burglar may or may not attempt to silence the bell. Burglars, when recalling the loud alarms, indicate that the sound itself is highly unnerving, and that their usual response is to make a hasty exit.

Alarm systems can be "beat" in several ways. The simplest way is to use a brace and bit plus a keyhole saw, to open up a panel of the door. In this way, entry through the door can be gained without opening it. Burglars know that doors are bugged in such a way that

6. The writer was able to visit a large detection agency headquarters. Access to the back room, where the panel of lights is constantly watched, was gained via the manager's password only. Two heavy locked doors separated the panel from the front of the building, where safes and security boxes were sold. The manager then proceeded to explain the operation of the alarm system, its mechanical dimensions, and how criminals attempt to "beat" it. His explanation, as well as his description of criminal techniques, was in substantial agreement with that given by burglars themselves.

a small switch (similar to the switch for the dome light in a car, which is closed when the door is opened), located in the door frame on the hinge side, is closed when the door is opened. It is an axiom for burglars in a bugged building not to open doors or to swing open low partitions set up in hallways. I was asked by one burglar to note functionally useless swinging partitions in hallways; it was his contention that they are allowed to swing freely only after hours, and that they are invariably bugged. The burglar walking down a hallway must go either over or under such a partition. If the construction of the door or partition is of poor quality, the button on the alarm can sometimes be kept in a depressed state by the insertion of a penknife blade.

A bugged window is easily identified by the strip of alarm tape around its edges. None of my respondents suggested any means whereby windows such as this can be beat. It was assumed, however, that not all windows will be bugged; consequently the burglar will check basement windows or windows fairly high off the ground, as well as skylights. My respondents agreed that skylights are frequently not bugged—a fact that burglars find puzzling, since they prefer to work on the roof of a building. The roof provides considerable privacy for their work—also, it was agreed, skylights tend not to be very securely fastened or constructed.

An alternative is to enter by the roof itself. This involves the use of a drill and a saw. Cases related to me included only situations of flat roof construction.

In addition to the possibility of avoiding the alarm, roof entry offers another advantage. Many alarms have their control box in the space between the ceiling and the roof. Access via the roof puts the burglar into a position where he can, if he is technically competent, "jump" the alarm, that is, cross the wires in such a way as to bypass the alarm mechanism or otherwise render it useless.[7] From then on, the burglar can proceed with relative freedom, although he must, of course, watch for the loud alarm that may be used in addition to the silent.

7. At this point the detection agency disagreed with the burglars' claims. The agency claimed that their alarms cannot be jumped—this will alter the "pulse-rate" of the current flowing through it and set off the alarm. Several burglars indicated the need to keep constant the length of wire through which the current flows, but added that this can be done by jumping the alarm with a coil of wire roughly as long as the wire used in the building. This calls for an accurate estimation of the wire used.

That "beating" alarm systems separates the men from the boys was made very obvious by my respondents. Most burglars recalling their experiences would intersperse their comments with statements such as, ". . . unless of course it's bugged, then I wouldn't touch it." Burglars unwilling or unable to cope with bugs must avoid them, thus confining their work to places other than major commercial buildings and establishments. As might be expected, burglars compare various localities in terms of the proportion of business establishments that are bugged.

Making the "in" constitutes a challenge and accomplishment in itself, aside from whether or not the caper is economically successful.

WHAT WAS THE BIGGEST THRILL ON A NIGHT WHEN YOU WENT OUT TO BLOW A CAN? I don't think I ever—I was rather clinical in my approach to these things. I don't think I ever actually experienced any particular kick at any time, but if there would be any one time of a moment of danger, as it were, it would be the actual making of an in —because of, well, in burglary—well, you can't—it's—you likely have to make a forcible entry, and the in is the all-important thing, and if there is any one moment of real apprehension and tension, you know—a feeling of being keyed up, and aware of everything that's going on, it would be at that time. Although for me, personally, I've never experienced it to that degree that I've heard other people express. (no. 27)

C. ACCESS TO CASH

The burglar interested in cash will not find it easily available, even after having entered the building. In commercial establishments, he may find it in the expected places, such as safes, cash registers, or in deliberately unexpected places, such as one shoe box among several hundred others. In residential dwellings, the burglar's task may be even more difficult, since the places where cash may be found are less predictable. A home does not have a cash register, nor, necessarily, a safe. Therefore, the burglar must make quick interpretations as to the most probable location of cash. The mental activity here is really a game of wits—of operating on the basis of reciprocal expectations. He proceeds on the assumptions he has regarding routine family behavior, and he anticipates uniformities in architecture as well as in styles of placing valuables. He may be frustrated by unexpected variations and leave empty-handed.

The burglar who works the commercial establishments faces quite different problems from those of the hotel burglar. He probably knows, prior to the burglary, where the cash is kept—he need not look for it; he need only obtain possession. Again, the difficulty of the task varies with the degree of technological sophistication. My respondents agreed that most older-type cash registers can be sprung by prying with a good screwdriver. They also agreed that today not much money is kept overnight in such registers.

The difficulty of gaining access to cash inside a business establishment necessitates a number of subspecialties of burglary. The most common of these is safecracking, which I will discuss in detail later. The use of self-serving vending machines has, however, introduced another source of cash, more easily available to the burglar:

> We did the juke box, pin ball machines, and stuff like that, and the money out of the cash register—anything we could, we took it. And these are about the easiest things to get into. Because the juke box— it's only got one lock. That takes the panel out—you can pull the panel out at the corner with the screwdriver and pop the lock, and on the side it's got the change. The only thing holding it is four head screws. And it only takes a second to take those out and then you get the money. It takes a minute to pop the shuffle board or something like that. You put in your screwdriver and you break the lock. You—on one we got eight hundred dollars out of three of these. So there's a lot of change in them. We done many in each. (no. 10)

The technical skills here are minimal, yet require some know-how, particularly for purposes of efficiency and speed. The tools required, though few and uncomplicated, are of a special kind—not those normally carried by a burglar:

> But mainly we work with a hammer, a screwdriver and a little pinch bar. And I take four screwdrivers, different sizes, 'cause each one you use is different. DIFFERENT KINDS OF SCREWDRIVERS? Phillips and—mostly Phillips, and the small little thin one, regular blade, that's what you need. Two Phillips and two regular screwdrivers, but one small one. WHAT'S THE SMALL ONE FOR? Well, in case you get like—in some of these change boxes, you get small Phillips, they won't fit, 'cause they're really small. So you have to use it. It's a special Phillips, a small one. (no. 10)

For more detailed analysis, we will look at what is probably the most complex type of burglary for cash: safecracking. Involving both entry to the building and entry into the safe or vault where the cash is kept, safecracking exemplifies the continuing war of technological escalation between the safecracker and the potential victims.

I have indicated earlier that all safecracking involves those skills necessary for a B & E. A glance at prison records indicates the prominent listing of the offence legally known as "breaking and entering." It may refer to a drunken kick-in or a sophisticated safecracking operation. The official charge itself does not specify such major variations in procedure; it does not indicate the degree of sophistication used, but simply the fact of forcible entry with or without theft. Procedural variations may be indicated in the police M.O. (modus operandi) report, and may play a part in sentencing considerations; however, none of this is indicated in the FPS (Finger Print Serial) record, even though some of it may be inferred from the type of sentence imposed. The official charge may simply be recorded as "B & E."

The safecracker occasionally employs someone to handle the entry for him, but it is generally assumed that safecrackers are also able to do B & E's. In our conversations, safecrackers seldom mentioned the techniques of entry, whereas persons who referred to themselves as "B & E men" would elaborate on these techniques. This does not mean that B & E techniques are taken for granted by safecrackers, for they must be regarded carefully; however, they are only a part of a larger and more difficult operation, namely the safeopening itself. The following analysis is based on descriptions by, and interpretations of, those convicted of this offence.

D. SAFECRACKING AS A SPECIFIC EXAMPLE

1. Introduction

My description of procedure will require increasingly specific descriptions of safes and vaults. Safecrackers differentiate between what might be called "strongboxes" (for example, light-gauge metal boxes that can be pried open) and the more heavily constructed safes. They distinguish between "easy cans" (or "tin cans") and more difficult ones, frequently by reference to the brand name of the safe. Although to the uninitiated the name "Chubb" may mean little, to a safecracker this name, coupled with the adjective "round," indicates a very difficult safe to open. "Round" refers to the shape of the door, and round doors are considered more difficult to open than square or rectangular ones.

The designation "safecracking" is a general term that includes both safeblowing (by use of explosives) and other methods of safe-opening. To distinguish between complex and crude methods, the derogatory term "safebreaking" may be used.

The following discussion focuses almost exclusively on the mechanical aspects of safecracking. From an analysis of my interviews, it is evident that the mechanical aspect of the actual opening of the safe is of central importance to the safecracker: this is exclusively *his* skill. He shares with other burglars the skills needed for making the "in," as well as those required for casing purposes. As for the latter, I will indicate in Chapter 6 how casing for purposes of safecracking has slightly different dimensions than when done for purposes of general burglary.

Before describing the various techniques used, a discussion of the source and nature of basic tools and equipment is in order.

2. Basic Tools and Equipment

The basic ingredient around which safeblowing techniques revolve is that of "grease" or "oil," the criminal's terms for nitroglycerine.[8]

(a) *Grease:* The older safecrackers refer back with some nostalgia to the days when grease was readily available in the form of dynamite sticks. These sticks "you could pick up any place." (no. 32) The "picking up" consisted of the theft of dynamite from construction sites or land-clearing operations. Dynamite sticks were apparently stored in temporary sheds on location. Safecrackers would drive out to these sites at night, pry open the usually poorly constructed doors, and take the dynamite sticks with them.[9] The sticks themselves were of no value for safeblowing, but the nitroglycerine the sticks contained was, and needed to be separated from the bonding compound which kept it in stick form. I was told this could be done in several ways:

8. The connotation of the term is obvious—nitroglycerine, being partly composed of glycerine, is, in fact, an oily substance.

9. In addition, they would take the fuses and detonators ("knockers") discussed later on p. 64.

You could take the nitroglycerine right out of that—by a process, putting it in a sack and then squeezing it out of the packing compound—can't remember the name of it—sort of like a moss—say sawdust or something. You could get the nitroglycerine right out of that. (no. 32)

Another account:

HOW WAS THAT DONE? Well, you used to be able to buy dynamite that didn't have a gelatine compound in it. The same as it is now. You —and you would just take it in a container of boiling water—you'd take the casings off the dynamite and you'd put it right in, and the heat separated the sawdust, the body—it wasn't a gelatine, but whatever it was. That is, whatever it was that held it together. The heat would just dissolve that and grease—nitro is heavier than water and, and it would sink right to the bottom. And you'd pour off the water, and there it is.

AND I UNDERSTAND THAT CAN'T BE DONE ANYMORE. No, no—they have a compound in dynamite—it won't dissolve in boiling water. It won't dissolve from the nitro itself. WAS THAT DONE DELIBERATELY? Well, I suppose it was partially done deliberately, yeh. To stop it—heh. That was definitely one of the factors, and it also made the—it—there may be a safety factor involved too. (no. 36)

As the above quotation indicates, legislation was introduced requiring a new bonding process for the manufacture of explosives. This process does not permit the separation of the nitroglycerine from the bonding compound, at least not by any methods known to safecrackers. Safecrackers referred to this new form of explosive as "gelignite" and "forcite." It is useful to them in its stick form only, and only for blowing a vault ceiling.[10]

Safecrackers disagree as to the motive for the change. Some are convinced the procedure was specifically designed to frustrate their own procedures; others feel it was for reasons of general safety.

But the Mounted Police are the ones primarily responsible, and the CIA or whoever was involved, you know. 'Cause everybody was taking the nitroglycerine out of dynamite. WHEN DID THIS HAPPEN, THIS CHANGE? When did the switch occur? Well, it occurred while I was in jail so there would be a kind of gap, but I would say, '42–'45—during that two-year period. I've heard different speculations on who actually

10. Although blowing a vault is a considerably different operation from that of safeblowing, it is considered to be within the "legitimate" domain of safecrackers.

made the first nitroglycerine, you know, by the chemical process. (no. 32)

A description of the chemical production of nitroglycerine was provided by each of the safecrackers interviewed. Each of the accounts was consistent in principle, although it was obvious some were able to provide dimensions others could not. This was generally consistent with their claims as to expertise and experience.

The basic procedure was presented cryptically as follows:

> (MAKING THE GREASE:) . . . like you add sulphuric and nitric acid and glycerine—that's all you need. And—but the thing was to get them in the right proportion. And we learn't this right proportion and from then on you could go to any drugstore and buy—separate drugstores—you could go to any drugstore. You wouldn't go and buy all three in one drugstore—you'd be asking for trouble. But go to one and buy the nitroglycerine, go to the next one and buy nitric acid, go to the third one and buy sulphuric acid. And keep them in a controlled temperature—this is the secret, keeping it at a controlled temperature. (no. 32)

Important issues are introduced here: how is the technical procedure learned, when does the purchase of merchandise arouse suspicion, and what are the consequences of making nitroglycerine?

Learning how to make grease is achieved via instruction by others, through reading, or both:

> HOW DID YOU LEARN TO MAKE THE STUFF? Oh, I'd heard about it— the thing that I actually studied was the *Encyclopædia Britannica*— they've got a very good run-down on it (laughs). Look it up and you'll find about three pages on it. (no. 32)

The following indicates how both the old and new methods were learned:

> OKAY, NOW TO REVIEW. YOU'VE BEEN LIVING OFF BLOWING CANS FOR TWO YEARS. Uh huh. WHAT KIND OF RELATIONSHIP DO YOU HAVE WITH OTHER SAFECRACKERS? DID YOU MAKE YOUR OWN GREASE ALL THIS TIME? No, we started to learn—you pick these things up from other safe-blowers and so on and so forth and finally I found out an old safe-man —he's dead now—and he was going out to make some grease. So now—and I told him I'd help him. "I'll get the powder and you take me out. I'll help you and you show me how to make it." He agreed. And he went with me—both of us went together, and, but like you say, the grease—we—I learned how to boil plastic, dynamite, say—how to

get grease out of it and then right after the war we learn't the chemical formula. HOW DID YOU LEARN THAT? It was passed on and it come out of some book. I don't know—a lot of safeblowers passed it on down the line, where you would buy these three ingredients and mix them together and you'd get grease. (no. 29)

Although it is legitimate to purchase the necessary ingredients, the motivation of such a purchase may be called into question:

YOU SAY YOU CAN BUY THE COMPONENTS PERFECTLY LEGALLY? I used to pose as a school teacher. I would even get them to give me a receipt bill and—so I could collect from petty cash, you see. There was some degree of restrictions on buying this—not legally, but simply on account of the product it is, you see. They are dangerous acids, actually. DID YOU BUY BOTH THE NITRIC AND SULPHURIC ACID YOURSELF? Oh yes. I HEARD THAT SOME OF THEM HAVE ONE GUY BUY THE NITRIC AND THE OTHER THE SULPHURIC. That's been done too. Well, originally I would walk right in and buy both in the same place, but as it became known a little bit that—amongst the authorities, well I would buy one in one place and the other in another, and then, particularly when —————— got caught with two of the components, and got convicted, then I would only buy one component at one time and take it and plant it and go back—I would never have two components at one time, in possession. (no. 26)

Another:

I SEE. UH HUH. DO YOU HAVE ANY TROUBLE BUYING THE STUFF? Well, the one—the tough one is the nitric acid, you know. Druggists will hesitate—sulphurics are comparably easy to get because there are so many valid reasons to use it, you know. But the nitric is difficult at times. SO WOULD YOU BUY A LITTLE BIT AT A TIME, MAYBE? No—the wholesales are fairly good, they. . . . (no. 32)

The following is an example of how these three ingredients are combined to make grease:

LET'S SEE, WHEN YOU MAKE THE STUFF, HOW MUCH WOULD YOU MAKE AT ONE TIME? Oh, on the average, you—when you buy, say nine pounds, that's the measurement even though it's liquid, you buy nine pounds of sulphuric acid, say—it comes in a big glass Winchester, you know. And then you go to a different drugstore, different place, you know, for six pounds of nitric—that gives you that 3–2 ratio, see what I mean? You got it all premeasured. YEH. And then the glycerine—the glycerine ration is usually one: 3–2–1. But it actually doesn't mean too much because the acid will only take so much glycerine and you can see it by watching how much it will absorb—see what I mean? You just throw the rest of the glycerine away.

The more time you take in this, the better. Not only safer, but you come up with a better product. And the dangerous aspect is where you add the glycerine—that's when, what's the chemical term? Fusion, you know; like actually nitroglycerine—like sulphuric acid is used to extract the water element from glycerine and from nitric acid. They make—just like the name implies—*nitro*-glycerine. The sulphuric acid is a kind of a, like a working agency, taking this water out and combining the nitric and . . . CATALYST? Catalyst, that's it. That's right.

The only baffling part that's found real difficult, when they make this, you know, "in"—say Duponts, for example—recognized manufacturer (LAUGHTER). This glycerine is injected right into it in some terrific airpressure somehow—now you haven't got that kind of resource available. Now this glycerine's got to be added. Say you got a five-gallon crock and you have that—you keep going around very slow—if you ever dropped it in there, well, it'd be (LAUGHTER) disastrous—oh god, I'm telling you! But you have to pour very thin, just the size of a needle, and you get to—you got to keep moving, keep it moving so, and you have a dairy thermometer, one of those big brass ones. You have that in your left hand and you keep stirring so there's no gobs of glycerine—you keep it spread out so there's a very thin layer. And you try to keep that ratio, because like, this catalyst operation is going on. You just keep adding at that rate. You do it by guess, but you learn fairly quick, 'cause you can see the —say there's a gob, for example, it gets kind of a rust color—you break it up with this dairy thermometer, you know—spread it out. (no. 32)

The key factor in making good grease is temperature control:

. . . you keep it as close as you can to forty degrees. Now if you go over you get poor grease; if you go under you get poor grease. And while you're mixing you watch this this thermometer, and if it's getting too cold you take it out of the ice for a few seconds and then put it back again. And you can make all of it in a hotel room, which I've done a lot. You can make it anywhere.[11] (no. 29)

The typical pattern was for one of the two partners in a safe-cracking team to be responsible for the grease. Safecrackers recog-

11. A common place to make grease was on the edge of a river, with the container located in shallow water. This kept the contents cool. The outdoor aspect also provided an element of safety, should the contents burst into flame.

nize that the quality of grease may vary from poor to good, depending on who makes it. Since a safecracker must be able to predict the explosive quality of the grease he is using, he will either make it himself, or get it from a reliable source.

The problems involved in purchasing the ingredients, the danger of being caught in possession of components, the unpleasantness of the noxious fumes emitted, and the danger of the procedure, plus the fact that one still might end up with poor grease, appear to have limited the production of nitroglycerine to a small number of safecrackers. All my respondents claimed to have been able to make it and implied that all safecrackers could do so. Several acknowledged they had made very little, and a few stated that they had made much.

> WELL, YOU SAY YOU ALSO PLANTED NITRO AROUND THE PLACE AND YOU MADE GALLONS OF THE STUFF, LITERALLY? Yes. DID YOU SELL IT? No—we used a lot and gave a lot away. That particular time—well, that was in '43, '44, and '45—a lot of very active burglars then, later on again, in the '50s, when I was here—it was the same thing, and I think I supplied most of them. (no. 27)

Another stated:

> NOW IF YOU SUPPLIED A MAN WITH NITRO FOR A BIG JOB, DID YOU GET A SHARE OF THE TAKE, THEN, OR . . . ? No, I've never done it that way —although that's been done. But it's not a general practice. Here again, it comes back to a rather unique and loose liaison among burglars. You know, if you've got something and I need something, and I haven't got it, there is generally no question about needing it, or getting something for nothing. (no. 32)

Although grease could be bought outright (at approximately one hundred dollars per ounce), it was more common for it to be replaced by the borrower, or for the supplier to be given a percentage of the take (usually five percent).

(b) *Soap:* A second ingredient for safeblowing is soap. Soap provides a funnellike structure through which the grease can be poured into the door of a safe. Like the components of grease, soap can be purchased perfectly legally. Unlike grease components, however, it can be purchased without arousing suspicion, and, therefore, without precaution.

Not all soap is equally good for safeblowing, and the desirable characteristics are not those generally advertised by soap companies. The soap must be malleable, and its consistency of the sort that will not permit the grease to drain through it. The only soap mentioned by name as meeting these requirements was the Fels Naphtha brand, although plasticine was mentioned as an alternative. The use of good soap is important:

> . . . now keep in mind, because now, there's **P & G** (Procter & Gamble) and there's all kinds of other soaps. Some of these can be really unsatisfactory. You can have, you know, grease coming down the door of the safe, you know—and things like that. It's pretty detrimental in blowing a safe—believe me. Because if it detonates up there you get a horrible report and nothing effective. (no. 32)

(*c*) *"Knockers" and string:* The grease must be set off by a detonator ("knocker") and the knocker in turn by a fuse or a spark from an electric source. The electric method is a more recent innovation, but all respondents indicated experience with both types. Before the use of electric knockers the ordinary fuse was commonly used. Even after grease could no longer be obtained from dynamite sticks, safecrackers would still visit construction sites to steal detonators and fuses. As with grease, the practice of getting them from other safecrackers, and replacing them later, was common. The fuse-type detonator consists of a small metal cap containing a small amount of fulmonite of mercury, and may be set off by a fuse placed inside the open end and crimped in place.

Although changes in the production of explosives made safecracking more problematic, some technical changes have been to the safecracker's advantage. The availability of electric detonators after World War II permitted the safecracker much greater control in the timing of his shots. The electrical detonator is closed on both ends and has two short wires protruding from it. Longer pieces of wire are attached, the ends of which are then touched to an electrical source. Subject to such contingencies as wartime, however, electric detonators have not always been easily available.

The following quotation indicates the functional advantages of the electric method, but also points out that the type used (whether electric or fuse-type) may be dictated not only by preference, but also according to their immediate availability:

> NOW, YOU SAID THERE WERE TWO KINDS OF WAYS TO GET THOSE DETONATORS TO GO OFF. ONE WAS ELECTRICAL AND THE OTHER . . . Yeh. Yeh, there's a fuse. WHEN DO YOU USE WHICH? Well, it's a matter of preference. I like the—well, I shouldn't say—I preferred the electric

because they're a lot quicker. I don't mean the actual action that takes place—they would—they're much more functional in the handling of them. You could time your movements so much better, whereas with the fuse, I don't know if you—well, we used to put them in and crimp them and make them fairly short, see? Because it burns so much feet per minute, see—depending on the type of fuse. We'd shorten the length, but it takes three or four matches; it takes rather an intense flame to start the fuse. You have to take the end of it and—and cut it back, you know—like a flower—to get at the central core of powder—that's just a black powder. It takes a rather intense flame to light it. And this takes more time, setting, than the electrical knockers. And—it's really much more functional. But sometimes, out of necessity, it depends on what you can either buy or steal. Ah—well, rock quarries were a favorite target. They always have a shack or a concrete, moveable building, where they store the stuff in, and sometimes they wouldn't have one type, you see. So it would depend on what you could get. We had plants of the stuff all over the country—as a matter of fact, I still got a lot. ———, I made him, I think, literally gallons of the stuff, and he had the worst memory of anybody I ever met in my life. (LAUGHTER) He'd always forget where he put it. (no. 26)

Forgetting the location of planted grease is only one of the problems associated with handling the basic equipment for safecracking. Contrary to what one might expect, however, transportation of grease was not considered dangerous. Only one of my respondents indicated a need to take particular care when transporting grease:

SO—IS IT DANGEROUS TO TRANSPORT (GREASE)? Uh—no, no. It's not really dangerous. What we did with it—it's like if I had a bottle, a medicine bottle, and if it was half full of grease I'd fill the other half full of water; now, grease won't mix with water. Now the water goes to the bottom and it cushions it—it keeps it from sloshing around. This is when it is dangerous—when it sloshes around. So, if you had a bottle, say with three ounces, and you use one ounce, you put another ounce of water in it. (no. 29)

The only precaution mentioned by the other respondents was associated with the illegitimacy of grease. For example, no more grease should be taken than is needed for the job, and grease should not be kept on one's premises—it is planted instead, which may mean literally burying it, or hiding it, usually outdoors.

The transportation of the knockers, particularly the electric type, is viewed as more problematic. Safecrackers do not like carrying them and agree they would never carry more than one per pocket. Another technique, not followed by all, is to twist the two wires of the detonator together before putting them into the pocket. They believe this prevents static electricity from setting off the knocker.

3. Techniques of Safecracking

Before we proceed to a discussion of specific techniques, some general information regarding safes will be useful. In addition to permissible variations or niceties in the techniques of safecracking, there are those slight variations demanded by differences in the make of the safe itself. Knowledge of these differences constitutes a good part of the informal discussion among safecrackers. It is on this basis that expertise and experience may be assessed. Thirteen different makes of safe were mentioned by various safecrackers:

> DO YOU WANT TO DISCUSS AT ALL HOW YOU IN FACT GO ABOUT UN-LOADING A CAN? Yeh, sure. First of all, it depends on the particular make. And, at that time the most prevalent make was the J. J. Taylor. And also the most convenient to blow, because of the structure of it. The many other types, Garry, Ford, Winnipeg, Hall—Marvin Hall. Oh, many of them. And they all—here again, through both experience plus talking to, you know, other pete-men, you discovered the peculiarities of each one. (no. 27)

The various makes are evaluated roughly in terms of the relative ease with which they can be opened. Some may also have meaning in terms of the specific technique required to open them, but generally the technique used is determined by other factors. The safecracker's ratings thus bear similarity to insurance company ratings (may, in fact, be determined by them), and it was not unusual for safecrackers to refer to a make and add, "It's got a high rating too," referring to insurance ratings.[12]

Because of technological change, the safecracker must constantly update his knowledge of safes. Twenty years ago, it was said that the three varieties of Hall safes were the easiest to open; today, the Hall safe is referred to as one of the most difficult.

---

12. That is, a safe with a high rating is more difficult to crack. The insurance rating also determines the cost to the owner of insuring its contents. For example, one safe company lists the cost of insuring five thousand dollars in a class one safe as being two hundred and sixty dollars, as compared with fifteen dollars in a class five safe.

Well, various doors are different. Now, the Garry—remember, I mentioned the red and black Garry . . . now, some of them are that thick, and the—well, safes are built for two reasons. One of them is burglar protection and the other is fire protection. And in order to combine the two in those days, it was a very difficult thing. So they got the maximum burglar protection that they could get, but the emphasis was on fire protection,[13] you know, for records, money, other valuables; and that door contained a fire clay, and so were the walls. That's the reasons for the varied thicknesses, depending on the actual purpose of the safe. And, today for instance, the Mosler is the toughest. The Chubb and the Mosler. They are built specifically for burglar protection, and fire protection secondary. (no. 27)

Safecrackers, like burglars, generally agree that, despite differences, there are basic similarities in all locking devices:

ARE SAFES ALL THAT SIMILAR, SO THAT IF YOU LOOKED AT ONE DOOR . . . ? No, they're not all that similar. They vary in the degree, yet the theory is the same. It doesn't matter whether it's a bank vault, or—or a safe door, the theory is just about the same in all. They keep coming up with new gimmicks to try and get ahead of us, and we come up with gaffs to beat their gimmicks! (LAUGHS) (no. 29)

The nature of escalation in the battle between criminals and property owners will be discussed later in this chapter. Also, before discussing the various techniques of forcibly opening a safe (namely, safecracking), another point must be made, having to do with the nonforcible, yet illegal opening of a safe.

It is assumed that for reasons of convenience office personnel develop short-cut ways of opening and locking safes. It is unlikely the door will be left entirely unlocked, but to leave it "on the hitch" ("day-locked," i.e., partially locked) during the day is not unusual. If left in this state overnight it becomes, of course, a convenience to burglars as well. To see whether or not the door is on the hitch the dial must be moved gently, one degree to the right, then one degree to the left, and so on, trying the handle each time. This is repeated to number four; after which it is considered not to be on the hitch.

The safecracker who has arrived prepared to blow the safe will, nevertheless, first try the handle to see if it is on the hitch or unlocked. One experienced safecracker recalled his embarrassment

13. "Safes, as known today, were introduced towards the end of the 18th Century, but these early safes only offered protection against fire." From *Too Late!*, issued by Chubb & Sons Safe Co. Ltd. (Leicester: Sceptre Litho Ltd.), p. 11.

when his novice look-out man turned the handle and opened the safe door while he was preparing to blow it open.

It is also assumed that safe combinations are easy to forget, and that this information is therefore to be found in a "permanent, yet handy place—in a desk drawer, on the back of a book or under a drawer." (no. 4) Whether or not a safecracker looks for this code depends on his casing results, on lighting, and on safety factors, including the need for speed. Looking for safe codes is seldom done, whereas trying the handle to see if the safe is on the hitch is standard procedure.

In the discussion below, the various procedures used in six basic safecracking techniques will be described. These techniques permit slight variations in procedure or style; however, the basic procedures are well known and understood by safecrackers.

(a) *The "jam shot"*: Of all explosive techniques, the jam shot is probably the most common. It is feasible on most safes, including those with either round [14] or square doors, and does not require the safe to be moved or laid on its back, as in the "Gut Shot." The following list of equipment and procedures has been assembled from my notes made during interviews with safecrackers:

Tools and equipment for the jam shot

(All tools, including the grease, must be assembled prior to going out on the job)

1. Soap, preworked [15] and wrapped in wax paper;
2. two ounces of nitroglycerine (grease) in graded medicine bottles—may be cushioned by adding water to the bottles (may take as much as four ounces);
3. a prefolded strip of cellophane;
4. heavy wooden matches;
5. detonator or knocker (not likely to carry more than two);
6. five inches of fuse "string" (several pieces) already crimped into the detonator, but not yet "split";
7. a razor blade;
8. a "fountain-pen" flashlight;
9. a pencil, if other than a jam shot is anticipated;

14. Round door safes, however, require two "shots": one done prior to the jam shot (known as "shooting for space"), discussed on page 73.
15. This preworking involves about fifteen minutes of hand-kneading, done at home prior to the caper.

10. an eighteen-inch crowbar;
11. gloves; and
12. old clothes (particularly pants and shoes) that can be discarded.

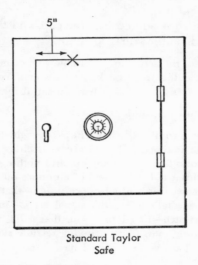

5"

Standard Taylor
Safe

Procedure for the jam shot

Step one: All equipment should be laid out on top of the safe. If the safe is too tall to make this convenient, some other nearby place must be found.

Step two: The piece of folded cellophane, original size four by eight inches is now folded into an eight by one-half inch strip. The length of the strip depends on the width of the door. For this reason, the safecracker should know the type and size of the safe before going on the job. Eight inches, however, is long enough for most safes. The strip of cellophane is then inserted lengthwise into the space between the door and the door-frame.

Step three: The preworked soap is fashioned into a cup with a funnel shape around the cellophane. This must be tight-fitting so that no grease will dribble down the front of the door.

Step four: When the cup is finished, the cellophane is carefully pulled out. This provides a channel for the flow of grease. Care must be taken not to jar the soap cup.

Step five: The knocker is placed in the cup, and the fuse is hung about three and a half inches over the edge of the cup. This provides about five seconds of time. Matches must be handy. A razor blade is then used to split the end of the fuse; this cannot be done beforehand, since the material in the center of the fuse may jar loose and the fuse not light properly.

Step six: The nitro is poured into the cup, and the operator must assess the rate at which the safe is "drinking":

> And this is where the actual art of safeblowing comes in—right now —is when you load this can, you know—this cup. You watch to see, like—just how fast this grease is—what you call drinking. (no. 32)

A little later the same respondent states:

> There has to be a continued chain, in effect, right to the detonator. If you haven't got it timed right the grease is either gone, and then all you get is a noise like a .38 going off, and nothing else. Or, if you shoot too quick you may have a third of an ounce outside in this cup, and only in effect two-thirds of an ounce inside—that's going to hang your safe up. Now, that's where the actual art is—in timing it. . . . That's what you watch—like I told you, that's the key part in safe-cracking, in watching that. If it's drinking terrible slow, for example, it may be a thick door; you see what I mean? (no. 32)

Step seven: The fuse must be lit[16] at a precise time also, because the knocker must go off just as the last of the grease leaves the cup. If the knocker goes off too soon, there will be too much grease left in the cup, and the door may be forced *in* rather than out. If the knocker goes off too late, all the grease will have drained away, and the knocker will go off without the grease going off. In both cases, there will have been noise, time and material will have been wasted, and the door will still be unopened. Furthermore, a second shot is always more problematic, since the amount of unexploded grease left in the can is not known. The unexploded grease will go off on the second shot; however, often its direction of force is not towards opening the door. Instead, it goes inward and tends, literally, to "burn the money."

Step eight: It is important to move about twenty feet away while waiting for the detonation. In actual practice, such precautions may not be feasible. In such cases, the safecracker simply crouches behind some furniture.

---

16. The fuse cannot be lit easily with ordinary paper safety matches; apparently, they do not produce enough heat. Wooden matches are used, and it usually takes several to light a fuse.

Step nine: Depending on the accuracy of the explosion, the door may need to be pried open, it may be blown off its hinges, or it may be swinging on its hinges. A number of contingencies arise when looking for the money. It may be burnt, or there may be a "Keister." [17] The safecracker does not expect to see bundles of cash openly before him; instead, he may be faced with stacks of paper, ledgers, and envelopes, usally placed in compartments of varying sizes. If he feels secure and does not suspect a "rumble," [18] he will sort the material on the spot, looking for money in ledger books, and so on. When speed is important, however, he must select, in addition to the cash itself, those items and records that he has learned from experience to have cash potential.

Step ten: The tools are left behind and exit is made from the building. Shoes and pants are removed and dumped into a garbage barrel. The clothing is discarded because brick dust[19] from the safe-explosions constitutes evidence for the prosecution.

The criterion of a perfect jam shot is that, after the detonation, the door must swing open on its hinges: "The hinges remain intact. A good safeblowing is with the safe doors swinging properly." (no. 32) The swinging door is in contrast to one that is simply "bulged," or one that is literally blown off its hinges. The difference has to do with the timing of the detonation and the amount and quality of grease used. If too little grease is used, the safe door is simply distorted or bulged. Besides probably having to attempt a second shot, the safecracker will probably use hand tools to attempt to pry the safe open. Safecrackers generally agree that a bulged safe is almost impossible to open by any method.

YOU'VE GOT TO USE JUST THE RIGHT AMOUNT? Just the right—you know, a different sized safe takes a little[20]—and then it depends on your grease, too. There's a lot of things that enter into this—who

17. "Keister" is the term used by safecrackers to refer to a small (usually round-doored) "safe within a safe." These small safes, designed for burglar protection, are frequently placed inside cheaper safes designed basically for fire protection.

18. "Rumble" refers to police intervention. To have a "rank" is to know that something has happened during the caper that is very likely to bring about police intervention.

19. Following the explosion the air is heavy with a very fine dust, resulting from the break-up of the firebricks that line the safe (for fire protection).

20. The standard Taylor safe (about four and a half by three and a half feet) is used as a gauge for determining how much grease to use. The Taylor safe requires one ounce of grease for a jam shot; a safe roughly twice its size would require two ounces.

made the grease, uh—how good you know it is. Because if you shoot
—if you attempt to blow a safe and you don't use enough grease you
are in a lot of trouble. (no. 29)

The use of too much grease "makes a bomb out of a safe." The
door may be blown off its hinges and shatter windows, thereby drawing attention to the scene. It increases the likelihood of the money
being burned and damaged. In the example below, a safecracker has
just recalled an early experience in which too much grease was used.

DID YOU KNOW RIGHT AWAY WHAT HAD GONE WRONG ON THE FIRST
SAFE? Well, we went back to a couple of safeblowers we knew and
we talked this over with them, and they explained to us exactly what
we had done wrong.

SO NEXT TIME YOU USE LESS GREASE? So we used less grease and less
grease as we went along until we found that we could blow a safe and
just have the door open instead of havin' it flyin' right off its hinges
and across the hall! (no. 29)

A common variation of the jam shot, preferred by some safecrackers, is to build two cups. The one at the top acts only as a funnel. The one at the bottom of the door contains the detonator that is
set off as soon as the grease drains down to it. This is described in
the example below, as is the procedure when using electric knockers
instead of the common fuse:

COULD WE GO THROUGH THE DETAILS OF HOW YOU IN FACT UNLOAD A
CAN? I used either a plasticine substance or naphtha soap. You knead
it up until it's a resilient piece, like putty, and starting about eight
inches from this corner you build a cup, like a spoon. I always used
to insert a little piece of cardboard in the crack of the door here,
and then adhere the cup to the door. And the reason I put the little
piece of cardboard in is so it wouldn't—seal off the crack in the door,
and then I would pull the paper out and take more putty and seal
up all this down to here, past that other point about eight inches
from the corner. There I would build another cup—same procedure
as the top.

Now, a J. J. Taylor is about the height of this desk. They were
generally fairly square, a Taylor, that is. And I would—I used to put
my grease in one of those bottles—you could buy them at the drugstore. They contain one ounce of liquid. And with this type of can
I would use slightly—oh, slightly more than half an ounce—I would
pour it in here, into this cup. You can see the action that would take
place. The bottom part of the cup is right at the very base of the crack

in the door. Consequently, it would funnel it into the crack. It would run down here. Now, the moment it showed up in the cup down below[21] I would have—uh—now, depending, now there are two types: the electric and the fuse—if I'm using an electric detonator, I would have everything ready. Detonator generally laying right on top of the safe. It has long wires to it, connected to a flashlight battery; and put the detonator in that. Put it in the cup and then fold the cup around the detonators—that's right in the crack there, and take the battery, touch the two ends there, and when you touch it, boom! It doesn't run out that way at all.

The use of electric knockers, plus two soap cups instead of one, removes some of the need for "the art of safecracking" referred to in the earlier method. It was my impression also, particularly from older respondents, that electric knockers have removed some of the "craftlike" qualities from the trade. At the same time, this improvement in safeblowing techniques has not compensated for the technological improvements in safe construction.

(*b*) *Shooting for space:* The "shooting for space" technique is used on smaller, usually round-door safes that are often located inside larger safes, and on those doors having small pressure bars that do not permit a jam shot. It is also used on the small cylindrical safes that are encased in cement and found in the floors of service stations and near the front of supermarkets. Where the door is horizontal, as in floor safes, the safecracker may simply pour a small pool of grease on it, near the center. This is then detonated. That is, on horizontal doors, it is not necessary to build a soap cup. For this reason, a standard-size office safe with a round door may, if possible, be tipped over on its back and worked on in this way.

On vertical round doors a soap cup is built up right on the face of the door, in the center, and detonated as in a jam shot.

> You're going to dish that door, no matter how well it is constructed, and it's going to get a severe enough jar from this shot to give you enough space to shoot. (no. 30)

That is, the "space shot" is to dent or "dish" the door enough to permit a standard jam shot. Safecrackers generally agree that round doors ordinarily fit too snugly to permit an immediate jam shot.

21. According to my respondents, nitroglycerine has certain properties that make it easy to see under these conditions. I was told that it will "gleam like quicksilver" under the ray of a pen-light.

Having to shoot for space means that one has to shoot twice; the disadvantages of this will be developed in our discussion of "harnessed safes," below.

The use of the tube-type safe (often referred to as "cannon-ball") has been frustrating for safecrackers accustomed to more conventional types. An older respondent stated:

> They're starting to use these tubes, in the floor, you know, in the concrete. And, well, I was familiar with these old brands. These can be blown, but in the course of it, I know, ———— and I, I don't know —we blew up, I don't know how many—how much money. Just shredded bills, you know. . . . through a rather hit or miss, but well, I really don't know too, I really don't want to talk too much about these. In my day it was different and I really don't know too much about. . . . (no. 27)

Martin, in his book, states:

> Now, there's one or two makes of safes that it don't pay the average guy to look at twice. A Diebold. And another one that is on the same order—a cylinder safe, constructed so that you can't punch it, can't strip it. The only way you can get into it is to blow it, and to blow it you're gonna have to take five or six shots. It's not practical to fool with.[22]

Another respondent who has done some safecracking stated:

> Cannon-balls, in concrete, near the front windows—you can't touch them, but I've seen 'em done, on a foggy night—wait for a good rainy night. . . . It makes an awful lot of noise and you might have to blow two or three times. (no. 15)

(c) The "gut shot": The "gut shot" is sometimes referred to as "Spindle Shot." Tools and equipment for the gut shot include a sledge hammer, soap, a pencil, two ounces of nitroglycerine, an eyedropper (may be part of the medicine bottle containing the grease), cotton batten or a strip of cloth, an eighteen-inch crowbar, knockers, fuse, a razorblade, gloves, and old clothes that can be discarded.

The use of the gut shot is limited because it requires that the safe be tipped over on its back. Once tipped, the equipment is placed on top of it, leaving room to knock off the dial:

> SO, THAT WAS THE GENERAL PROCEDURE THEN? Uh-huh. WELL, THAT'S ON WHAT YOU CALL A JAM SHOT? Now—this here's your dial. Now you

22. J. B. Martin, *My Life in Crime*, New York: Signet Books, 1952, p. 85.

knock this off. That's just one blow with the hammer, and you tip the whole safe over on its back. Then you take an eyedropper, and the nitro will follow the path down. See—it's lying on its back, actually. NOW WHAT KIND OF A SHOT IS THIS CALLED? Gut shot. And the gravity will pull the nitro and this is called the gut box, for very obvious reasons. 'Cause the—it contains the actual mechanism—the tumblers.

Well, anyway—the gravity takes the grease down the spindle and it can't go any further, and you just pour it with the dropper. Well, the most that you would use is a dropper and a half. That's all. And then you just lay your detonator right across it—oh, probably you build a little bridge, you know. Just sort of to form a cup, and you just put the cap in there, and boom! You let it go—with an electric detonator, you see.

AND WHAT DOES THAT DO TO THE MECHANISM ITSELF, INSIDE? Well—it just destroys it all. You see, the locking mechanism—you know, the way it works is a series of—well, let me draw it. You see, a series of tumblers and a locking bar comes over here directly, you see. There'd be three here and they go into holes in these cams. See?

WELL, HOW LONG WOULD IT TAKE YOU TO DO A TAYLOR, FROM THE TIME YOU START TILL IT'S OVER? Oh, about four to five minutes. DID YOU DO IT ALL BY YOURSELF, OR DID YOU HAVE SOMEONE WITH YOU? Oh, generally—generally, I had someone with me, but by my nature I generally done the work. (no. 27)

The single advantage of the gut shot as opposed to the jam shot is that it can be used when the door of the safe is very snug or has "lips" that do not permit the jam shot. (Square-type doors are not easily "dished.") It also has several disadvantages. First, the safe must be in a position where it can be tipped over, and, secondly, knocking off the dial involves several sharp blows with a heavy hammer—the noise of this operation would not be advisable in some situations. This shot is also susceptible to misfiring; as in the jam shot, the safe may "drink" too quickly or too slowly. It is sometimes possible to stuff a rag soaked with nitroglycerine, into the "gut-box." This prevents the explosive from draining away from the mechanism.

(d) *"Harnessed" safes:* The jam shot is designed for the least technically sophisticated safes; it requires sufficient space between the door and the door jamb (frame) for the grease to enter. The effectiveness of the jam shot prompted several mechanical improvements in the manufacture of this type of safe. One of these improvements provides a small trough or "lip" on the steps of a safe door, to catch the grease near the outside edge of the door. A more important and mechanically more complex change has been the introduction of pressure bars. Heavy chrome rods that can be seen on the outside of the safe door, pressure bars are moved into their own sockets after the door has been closed, and provide a wedge effect that pushes the safe door into its frame very tightly. Safecrackers refer to safes with pressure bars as "harnessed" safes.

The net effect of pressure bars is to make the introduction of nitroglycerine by the jam shot impossible. Before the jam shot can be used, the pressure bars must first be loosened or removed. This is done by an initial explosion at a vital spot on the pressure-bar mechanism. If the shot is successful, it will be possible to proceed with the usual jam shot.

Safecrackers do not think of mechanical improvements per se as constituting a serious threat to what they can do with nitroglycerine:

> Actually, you could beat any style of vault with nitroglycerine—I don't care about that. However, the time element and the noise element are the ones that beat you. (no. 32)

Safe manufacturers and safecrackers both generally agree that any safe can be blown with nitroglycerine. The whole point of technical improvements is to make the task more time-consuming and more difficult, rather than mechanically impossible. To the safecracker, the problem of pressure bars is one of *noise*. As stated, a safe with pressure bars requires a minimum of two shots of grease. The first shot is to loosen the pressure bars; the second is to open the door itself. Technically, the procedure is very similar to that required when "shooting for space." It is the second shot that is problematic because of noise:

> WHY DID YOU WANT THEM ON A MAIN STREET? Well, on a main street a noise can go unnoticed. . . . Like, it's amazing—like, it's a general understanding you can shoot one shot any place. . . . The policemen might be on the beat and hear that, but it's a real hard sound to locate. It's almost impossible to tell, even which side of the street it's on. He knows there's a safe being blown somewhere, but where? You know what I mean? YEH. It's when you start having to shoot two or three times—this happens, you know. But then you're in trouble. (no. 32)

The noise of traffic, a bother to most persons, is an advantage to the safecracker, whose concern is directly opposite that of the house burglar. The latter prefers total silence, because if he is on the "live prowl" he wants to be able to hear the occupants in order to assess their state of sleep, or anticipate any movements.

> "Oh no! That's the worst part. You don't want no noise. 'Cause I wanna hear everything, so if somebody wakes up you're going to hear it. If there was a lot of noise they'd get up and you'd never know, probably." (no. 21)

If he is not on the live prowl, he wants to be able to hear anyone coming near or entering the house. Besides safecrackers, persons involved in kick-ins (particularly in small towns where businesses are not bugged) prefer noise, so that their own noisy operation will be less noticeable:

> As for time, a night of rain and thunder is best. Wind, rain and thunder obscure noise and people are likely to stay home. (no. 44)

The literal kicking-in of a door is not heard above the noise of wind and rain. I was also told that on a stormy night one can break window panes without fear of attracting attention.

(e) *Nonexplosive techniques:* The safecracker is not limited to the use of explosives. Depending on noise factors, make of safe, and the availability of equipment, he may or may not use explosives. Nonexplosive methods take three major forms: "peeling" ("unbuttoning" or "stripping"), "punching a can," and drilling a safe.

Peeling, which can be used only on cheaply constructed safes, consists of driving a series of wedge-shaped chisels of ever increasing size into a spot between the door and the door jamb, or between the safe wall and the strip of angle iron riveted over each corner of the safe. When a hole has been created large enough for the entry of a heavy steel bar, the safecracker proceeds to pry loose the door covering, or, in the case of the corner angle iron, he pops the rivets one by one. If he is working on the door, he will continue this procedure until he can reach in and manipulate the mechanism. If he is working on the corner of the safe, he will remove a complete side panel until he can work at the weaker inside wall with an axe or other heavy, pointed object.

This procedure is similar to a variety of technically uncomplicated methods used on cheaply constructed safes. A safe may be upended and the bottom cut out with an axe. Acetylene cutting torches have also been used, but constitute difficult transportation problems.

They are used frequently when the entire safe is stolen by the burglar, in which case he has time to work on it elsewhere at some leisure and with safety.

Peeling is no longer considered a viable form of safecracking.[23] Safecrackers agree that poor quality safes are still in considerable use; however, they are not used for keeping what the safecracker considers worthwhile amounts of money.

A second nonexplosive method is "punching." Next to the jam shot and the gut shot, this is probably the most popular method of safeopening. Its use is confined to relatively unsophisticated safes, but it is a feasible method on most safes that are amenable to either the jam or the gut shot. The tools required for "punching a can" are: a heavy hammer and a long, high-quality steel punch with a narrow tip.

For convenience, the safe should be tipped over on its back, if possible, before the work begins. The dial is knocked off with a few hard blows of the hammer and the safecracker then knocks the spindle down with punch and hammer. This is difficult, but safecrackers insist it can be done even on good-quality safes. The spindle is knocked down (or in) until one can hear the tumblers, which rotate on the spindle, fall. At this point, the handle will be tried—if the spindle has been punched in far enough, the door can be opened simply by turning the handle.

This procedure offers several advantages, the most important being the ease with which the equipment necessary for the job can be obtained. The equipment can either be bought for very little money or easily stolen. Several prisoners indicated that a natural "first" crime for newly released prisoners is to "punch a can" in a garage. By using the tools already in the garage, no initial cash outlay is required, and the danger of stealing the equipment is avoided. Secondly, safecrackers disregard the noise of this operation. I was told that the noise of the hammer does not carry much beyond the building, and, if it does, people consider it to be a legitimate noise.

A third nonexplosive technique, "drilling," is quieter than using

23. Safe manufacturers caution against the use of older-type safes that can be peeled: "In 1835 Charles Chubb patented the first burglar resisting safe and from this time until the 1890's safes consisted of a rectangular box made from steel plates riveted to an angle-iron frame. . . . Unfortunately, to break into the majority of these safes it is simply a matter of finding the first rivets and peeling off the back and sides." From *Too Late!*, Chubb & Sons Lock and Safe Co. Ltd., p. 11.

explosives—in some situations an important advantage—but more time-consuming, difficult, and uncertain.

> It's a lot of hard work, drilling. It's a steady hour of pushing and pushing and you never know whether you'll make it or not. (no. 15)

Although some of the cheaply constructed safes are opened by drilling, they are generally not considered worthwhile because, as in the case of those that can be peeled, "big" money is not usually kept in them. To open them, a hole is drilled near the dial, and the tumblers are manipulated by wire or finger.

The more expensive or better built safes are more complex. Safecrackers agree that the quality of the steel used in modern safe construction renders them impervious to drilling, except in what is known as the "soft spot." None of my respondents claimed ever to have opened a good safe by drilling; the soft spot, it was said, can be located only with the aid of information from someone involved in safe-manufacturing or repairing. Respondents express great admiration for those who do successful drill jobs, but do not recognize these criminals as part of the safecracking fraternity. According to newspaper accounts, the practice is current, though infrequent.

> Maybe they worked where the safes are made or something, and they know how they're made, and they know where to drill them, you see. . . . you wouldn't know where to drill, but it's like everything else, eh? Guys gettin' more scientific at it, gettin' more thorough and —and these are about the only ones—the guys who've been workin' at safes, who can get in there. . . . (no. 14)

4. The Interpretation of Technique

The various techniques by which safes may be opened have implications for the division of labor, status allocation, and legal identification. Although the techniques that have been described can be performed by one person, it is more common for two persons to participate. Safecrackers refer to other safecrackers in terms of two-person groups or "partners." A fairly permanent liaison between two people, the partnership is recognized by other safecrackers. Each partner comes to assume certain safecracking responsibilities. Usually, one does the actual safecracking while the other acts as "point-man" (watchman); both, however, will be known as "safecrackers."

But really, the only reason you need two men is that one has to watch out, kinda be a look-out, like—if you're in a building, back in the office or something and you can't see out on the street, and you don't know who's walkin' around out there; might be a cop around or anything when you're ready to set off the explosion, so one guy has to be—make sure that everything is clear when it goes, you see. And that'd be the main reason for having two guys—if you were somewhere where you weren't worried about being heard or anything, you would easily do it yourself—but it's like everything else, you like company. (no. 14)

If a third man is needed for a specific caper, it is unlikely he will be recruited from among other safecrackers, but rather from among the general rounder population. He will be used as a point-man, rather than for the actual safecracking.

Safecrackers may specialize in certain techniques of safecracking, and each partner in a group of two may feel particularly competent in one specific technique. In such cases, the demands of the particular caper will determine who does what.

I WAS INTERESTED ALSO IN—LET'S SAY YOU ARE THREE FELLOWS AND YOU'RE GOING TO BLOW A SAFE. HOW DO YOU DECIDE WHO DOES WHAT? Well, you try to go, of course, this is a—lots of safecrackers are ego-centric and egotistical, you know. Lots of guys will, when you say, "I went out last night with so and so," they'll say, "well, what'd you go with him for, he don't know nothin, he couldn't do nothin, he don't know from nothin," whereas you might know in your own mind that the guy does know—the one that's doin' all the yakkin' doesn't know— it's somethin' you got to find out for yourself and by others—guys that have gone with him and they talk—each one cuts up him and him and him, and you know how good you are, and you tell. So if we decided, say three of us went out, and say we had never been out with each other before, say me and ———— and somebody else. Say we'd never been out together before. If we had been out with each other before, we would probably know which is, which should do the work—if we hadn't been we'd just have to rely on what we'd heard from other guys and of course we'd say, "Well—how are you at this kind of a shot? A spindle shot or a jam shot, or what do you think?" And he might say, "I don't think it should be done that way—I think it should be done this way."

And you would just kind of talk about it like this, and then some-body would have to concede and say, "Well, you go ahead and do it." I don't think there would ever be much of an argument there—there is the odd time you get a couple of guys that are real high on them-selves and there may be a little row about how you are going to do it, but most guys would step aside and say, "You do it." Like, I know ——— and I—if we would have went out together, in the old days, I know that ——— would have said, "Well, you go ahead, you do it —you know more about it—you do it." And I would probably say the same: "No, no—I think—I don't think I do—you go ahead and do it." And this is probably what would happen. We'd probably wind up tossin' to see who does it, or maybe we'd just both do it together. (no. 14)

The number of persons participating in a safecracking is an indication of the perceived difficulty of the job. A safecracker working alone will probably not be carrying a gun. He is not expecting trouble; if he were, he would not work alone, and he would probably pack a gun.

AND YOU WEAR GLOVES, I SUPPOSE? Oh yes, yes. DO YOU CARRY A GUN WHEN YOU ARE OUT ON THIS TYPE OF WORK? I have, yes, I have. ONLY WHEN YOU ARE BY YOURSELF, OR ALSO . . . ? No, not when by myself. No, I don't think I have when I've been by myself. But usually when I have there's been two or three of us. But then it's because of the type of premises.

DOES THAT MEAN THAT WHEN THERE ARE SEVERAL OF YOU THEN IT MEANS IT'S A PRETTY DIFFICULT SITUATION? Yeh, yeh. And I know when I went back East I joined up with a mob that—well, that's the wrong word to use—two or three people that were pretty high flying, and they took the ——— Bank, where grease was used—nitroglycerine was used, you see. And I think we had about three guns with us that night, plus a baseball bat, or softball bat. (no. 27)

A knowledge of the mechanical aspects of safecracking also provides a basis for the appreciation of the psychological rewards involved:

. . . as a matter of fact, I enjoyed this. This is the funny part of it —it isn't actually—when you—I don't know how to describe it. Oh, it's not an orgasm or nothing like this, but it *is* nice, say when you can knock—either punch the door off or blow the door off a safe and reach inside and take out a handful of money.

WHAT'S THE BIGGEST THRILL IN BLOWING A CAN? I imagine when that door swings open. AND WHAT ABOUT THAT DOOR OPENING—IS IT LOOKING AND SEEING THE MONEY? Oh yes, you're disappointed, but then you're satisfied too that you've got the door off—you've done the job, you know. What you're accomplished to do—you've done, and if you've done it well. . . . (no. 29)

During a social occasion I had with several rounders, the group had spent some time discussing the pleasures of gambling at Las Vegas, when one member said to no. 24: "what is it in safeblowing that gives you the biggest kick?" He replied,

> I guess it's when it goes off—the big bang—that's the most exciting part. Then when it (the dust) clears, to see if the door is open. That's the point—did it work? Does it open properly? Did I put in too much or too little? That's the big spot! (no. 24)

Someone asked whether the excitement over the door opening was not really a matter of curiosity as to how much money might be in the safe. To this he strongly objected: "Never! The money is secondary—you take what there is."

The statement below suggests that both the possibility of making a big score and the satisfaction derived from successfully opening the safe contribute to the excitement of the event.

> Now after I get inside, all my fear more or less is gone. And you concentrate on the safe, and you can look at it and—of course you always know what kind of safe it is before you make your entrance and everything. You go in, you got your tools and everything, and you can estimate what's in the safe. If it's a place that has delivery trucks, you can figure five hundred dollars per truck for every truck they got and they'll have that much in the safe. I mean that's the average for any kind of business whether it be a beer truck or a dry-cleaning place. But still in all, that jewel might be the one. It just might be the guy that's beating the income tax, or it might be the guy that's booking all the big football payoff or layoff or something. And there's no charge in the world, man, like when you see that smoke . . . For instance, if you're punching it and you hear that pin hit the back of the safe: "clinggg!" You know you're home free. Or if you're peeling it you see that smoke come out—whenever you pop that door and see the smoke you know that you've cracked the rivets and it's all yours. And when you see that safe door open, it is a *charge*. I think the most safes I ever made was six of them in one night. But that was four of them in one building—you just go from safe to safe. But man, it never became less. You know, it's not like screwing. The first time it's pretty wild, then each time it tapers off; you get part of the same drive, you know, the same action, but it's not like the first. A safe's not like that. Each time it's more so because you figure the odds are more in your favor of it being the big score.[24]

24. Jackson, "Who Goes to Prison . . . ," p. 55.

Another safecracker compared the satisfaction of safecracking to that of other manual skills:

> Well, referring now—actually to myself. The actual mechanics of particularly burglary. I'm a carpenter now, and a rather good one. I worked outside on that for several years. And I found that the same aspect that attracted me to this particular type of crime has actually been sublimated into carpentry work. Now, this is an actual experience, that I've known definitely works within myself. I get a creative enjoyment out of it. Now—this is destructive, actually, but still it's functional, and now that I'm—the same creative enjoyment is put into carpentry work. There's something creative about that.
> BY THE WAY—WHAT IS THE GREATEST THRILL IN SAFECRACKING? IS IT THE GETTING OF THE MONEY? No, I don't think I did it strictly for the money. (LONG PAUSE). With me, personally, it's been a—a lack of motivation, I think. I—uh, I tended to drift into this and (PAUSE) . . . then got myself involved in situations where I tended to rather react with a hell-of-a-lot of hostility and expressed my hostility in directing my energies in a criminal way. Fundamentally it wasn't money.
> WHAT WAS THE BIGGEST THRILL ON A NIGHT WHEN YOU WENT OUT TO BLOW A CAN? . . . I don't think I ever actually experienced any particular kick at any time, but if there would be any one time of a moment of danger . . . it would be the actual making of an in . . . (no. 27)

Another burglar with some experience in safecracking commented:

> Maybe—it may be just that it's crime, but I can tell you, that I've had no greater thrill than the first time that I opened a safe door. When I opened, you know—I went at it—I didn't peel it or nothing. I went at it in a sophisticated manner and it was a thrill. WHAT IS THE THRILL—IS IT THE FACT OF OPENING THE DOOR, OR IS IT THE FACT THAT THERE IS MONEY THERE? No, no—just opening the door—I wasn't worried about the other at that time. (no. 2)

It is clear from the above that the mechanical complexities and related hazards of safecracking make for a sense of achievement for those who manage the operation successfully. The various techniques are thought of not only in terms of economic gain but also in terms of mechanical expertise. A "beautiful job" is not necessarily a comment indicating that a large amount of money was taken; more probably it implies the appreciation of another's craftsmanship.

In this sense, the safecracker resembles the craftsman whose reward is more psychological than economic. On the other hand, since safecracking is very dangerous, it cannot be indulged in for pleasure only.

The technique of safecracking used by particular safecrackers is seen by others in terms of expertise and acknowledged by way of status allocation. It is seen as having meaning not only for safecrackers and other rounders, but for law enforcement personnel as well.

Each of the techniques described above is subject to numerous minor variations peculiar to the operator. The degree of safety (from the explosion) desired varies among safecrackers. Those who prefer to be in an adjacent room need longer wires for the electric detonators, and so on. Safecrackers believe that each safecracker develops his own particular style, and that the police can identify the operator by interpreting the technique after the event.

> M.O. is a big thing. M.O.?—I'M NOT SURE . . . Would you call it "modus operandi"? OH! And this is a big factor—uh—when you're learning how—maybe somebody shows you how to blow a can and you can blow it that way, and it works. Well, you got a tendency to always follow the same procedure because if it worked for you once you figure it will work for you again, so you always just—I might go in and knock the dial off the safe and put on a little cup and blow it through the spindle and I open it this way. ———— might go in and put soap in the top crack and open the door up, but you pretty well always do this the same way. Not only this, but the way you get into the place —how you break in—some guys will go in through a roof—another guy will flip a window and another guy has another way of gettin' in—maybe right through the brick wall or something, and they do this consistently—and the police can pretty well look at the job and say, "Well, so and so made it." They know—they *know*—just by the way everything is done.[25]
>
> WHY DON'T YOU CHANGE YOUR METHODS THEN? Ah—because if you go out fishin' and you put a big crazy kind of a spoon on and you throw it in and you get a real big nice steelhead, you'll continue to go back and do it again, because you figure you'll get another one. If it works for you once, you figure it's that important. For instance, you figure, "To hell with the lot—I don't care whether they knew I blew it or not, they're not going to get me with nothin' anyway," see?

25. A senior corrections officer at the Drug Rehabilitation Centre said, "The police will tell you that a lot of these guys, let's say four or five safes have been blown, the police can look at the jobs and it's just as if they've left their fingerprints—they know immediately who did it just by how it's done."

So what do I care? So if you figure you can open it in a certain way, you will, and of course—oh, hundreds of times I've had them come to me the day after and say, "Well, we *know* you got so and so—we *know* you got it," and you stand there laughin' and say, "So what? What if I did? What're you going to do about it?" They can't do nothin', 'cause they haven't got nothing—but sooner or later they will have something, you see? Maybe a footprint. (no. 14)

Despite his casual remarks regarding the police "knowing," the same respondent stated:

Now, once they know, say me and no. 32 blew a safe . . . now this really simplifies things for them because they just watch us and at the right time they nail us, maybe pickin' up the tools that we used at the place or maybe it's the money that we planted—maybe we kept the bills and planted the silver, or they catch us changin' ten dollar bills into hundreds or somethin', and some of them are marked, but the thing is—they know who did it and they got a big edge in nailin' us on somethin.' Now that's the best I can figure. (no. 14)

Safecrackers feel ambivalent toward carelessness in leaving fairly obvious identifying clues. They regard the habit with a mixture of respect and apprehension. One safecracker apparently had the habit of meticulously cleaning up after he had blown a safe, even to the point of dusting the furniture. Safecrackers asserted that his style was a dead giveaway to the police. At the same time, he was known for his ability not to leave evidence that would be admissible in court.

My respondents also pointed out that some techniques are more standardized than others, and less amenable to variations (for example, the spindle shot). In these cases, the visible effects would be quite similar no matter who did the shot. Safecrackers assume, however, that the police look for additional clues such as the type of an "in" made, the type of place victimized, and the location of the job, besides using their own knowledge of what various rounders are up to at any given time. In addition, the safecrackers readily admit that in terms of security they make their biggest mistakes *after* the caper, by telling others of their action:

. . . and conversation, I think would be the biggest factor—yeh, I think. Seems like nobody is able to keep this to himself so you get in a big crowd, a whole bunch of you, and you're yakkin', and pretty soon it gets to be common knowledge and all the safecrackers all over town know who did just about every score, you see? And, well, this is

alright if you was only talkin' amongst yourselves, but you get girl
friends and wives and other guys that aren't safecrackers and pretty
soon—I think it's just a matter of time before it gets back to the
police. (no. 14)

E. BEHAVIORAL IMPLICATIONS OF TECHNOLOGICAL CHANGE

The relationship of changing technology to the social structure
has been of central interest to sociologists. An old and ongoing
theme of special interest to those in the social-problems field has
been the effect of changing technology on employment. Related to
this, yet of more specialized focus, is the interest of industrial sociologists in the effect of technology on worker behavior and organization. Much academic as well as public and governmental concern
has addressed itself to the problems facing those being displaced by
technology.

It is understandable, nevertheless, that no such sympathy has
been extended to the criminal who finds himself displaced by technological advances. Such an attitude is no doubt partly owing to
the assumption that the criminal's loss is the public's gain. Further,
the criminal is generally viewed in moral, rather than occupational,
terms. Since we know so little about the mechanical and social skills
involved in the criminal's routine activity, we are in no position to
appreciate the effects of changes in these areas.

To say that the criminal, too, is affected by technological change
can hardly be called a discovery. It is perhaps more enlightening
to ask how the criminal responds to such change. The answer to
such a question might reveal interesting similarities and differences
between the effects of technology on socially approved activity versus socially *disapproved* activity. The criminal is not granted public
aid when faced with unemployment.[26] If he wishes to retrain himself
for other types of crime, he must do so on his own, and, furthermore, must do so in the face of obstacles deliberately put in his way.
The ongoing and escalating conflict between the criminal and his
potential victims may involve minor mechanical improvement as
well as major changes in security systems. For example, "loiding"

26. Unless, of course, we think of prison as a subsidized retraining program.
Prison programs are intended to retrain for legitimate occupations, but, as we will
show, may also be used for illegitimate ends.

a door was a very common method of opening locked doors some fifteen years ago and earlier. The method consists of inserting a stiff yet flexible piece of plastic (approximately two by four inches in size) between the door frame and the door latch. A recent and relatively cheap mechanical change in ordinary door locks now renders this method ineffective.

The effect of technological change on criminal behavior is particularly well exemplified in the case of safecracking. It can only be understood with the technical features of the safecracking process clearly in mind. A number of important technological changes have drastically altered both the safecracker's technique and his social patterns.

Although the early (1930–45) safecracking community thought of itself as constituting a social group in Vancouver even at that time, its cohesiveness had to do with the communication of information about police activity and about "scores" that only another safecracker could properly appreciate. The safecrackers were not held together by economic factors, nor was there any particular interdependence based on sharing skills or equipment.

The technical change from dynamite to other forms of explosives cut off the criminal's access to a simple and ready source of nitroglycerine, posing a serious problem for the safecracker. He faced several alternatives: one, he could revert to other forms of crime; two, he could restrict himself to safes that could be punched, drilled, or otherwise manually opened; or three, he could find new sources of nitroglycerine.

There is no way of knowing how many took the first alternative as a permanent step, though there are indications that at least some took it as a temporary measure. The second alternative was too restrictive and unprofitable. Most turned to new sources of the explosive.

Given the difficulties involved in making nitroglycerine, plus the demand for it, it is not surprising that some arrangement for the supply of ready-made grease would arise. Consequently, a loose form of specialization began on a fairly large scale. There is no indication that anyone made his living exclusively on making and selling grease, but several persons became known as ones who were likely to have a supply and who would be willing to sell it, or, in many instances, give it away with the understanding that it would be replaced at a later date.

This new form of economic cooperation between safecrackers strongly reinforced the already existing social bonds. The majority of the safecrackers were now dependent on each other for the source of their livelihood. Such dependence, furthermore, was not an impersonal buyer-seller relationship. Making grease was a legally precarious business, and the producer could safely sell or give only to proven customers.

Some safecrackers depended on their own resources and remained relatively independent, but these were exceptions. Potential safecrackers could enter the field only by winning the confidence of those in control of grease. Safecrackers remark on the great amount of borrowing, buying, and other interactions revolving around grease.

It may well be that the unintended consequence of making nitroglycerine more difficult to obtain has been to strengthen the criminal community. It enabled the leaders to screen new "recruits" and necessitated the development of a stronger subculture based on mutual aid and group loyalty.

Some technical changes have been in the safecracker's favor. The development of electrical detonators was of real advantage, for it permitted the safecracker much greater control in the timing of his shots. The safecracker has also been able to take advantage of better-quality tools and more advanced means of communication. He may even feel that in some respects he is ahead of his opposition:

> I took up radio—this all ties in with the way we work. As the police progress, we progress. If you don't, you're dead. Like, when they got two-way radios in their cars, we got two-way; we used walkie-talkies before the city police did. (no. 29)

However, the discussion on safecracking techniques has indicated how changes in safe design have made safecracking increasingly more difficult. Changes in safe design have been paralleled by changes in building architecture and in the location of safes. Modern design no longer relegates the safe to a back office. They are now to be found in full view, often flood-lit at night, near large plate-glass windows at the front of the stores. All of these changes have tended to frustrate the practicing safecracker and discourage others from taking up this line.

Informants agree that the two changes most injurious to burglary and safecracking have been the development of a credit economy, and the invention of night depositories.

The credit economy has resulted in fewer cash transactions; safecrackers complain that there just isn't much cash in safes anymore. Likewise, the night depository now makes it a simple matter for the businessman to deposit his day's take in the bank after hours, rather than putting it in his safe.

The development of night depositories coincided with complex burglar alarm systems, the most elaborate of which are to be found in banks. My informants agree that these technical developments have left only the most skilled criminals operating as safecrackers. Alarm systems and the credit-card systems have discouraged the burglary of major business establishments; banks, for example, are seldom burglarized today. For this reason, say my informants, the burglary of business establishments has given way to armed robbery. In the criminal as in the conventional context, the long-run merit of technological progess is questionable.

4

OVERT CRIMES
(VICTIM CONFRONTATION)

The Technical Dimensions of Robbery, with Special Attention to Bank Robbery

A. INTRODUCTION

The information received from the forty-five subjects interviewed for this study (see the appendix) includes comments on a wide variety of criminal behavior. Without wishing to provide yet another detailed typology of crimes, I believe it is useful to differentiate between those crimes committed surreptitiously and those involving direct confrontation with the victim. The one involves the taking of property without the owner's consent or knowledge, the other involves the demand for property and its being "given" to the thief by the victim. Roughly speaking, this follows the legal distinction between burglary and robbery. The primary difference sociologically is that robbery involves direct interaction between thief and victim, whereas burglary does not. It follows, therefore, that the skills associated with robbery must include those necessary for the management and manipulation of people. This is not to minimize the importance of mechanical and technical skills, but to indicate that victim confrontation adds an additional dimension to the skills necessary for success in nonsurreptitious crime. Sutherland points out that, in terms of status, professional thieves distinguish between those criminals whose work depends primarily on manual dexterity as opposed to those whose work depends on "wit, 'front' and talking ability":

> . . . burglars, robbers, kidnappers, and others who engage in the "heavy rackets" are generally not regarded as professional thieves, for they depend primarily on manual dexterity, or force. A few criminals in the "heavy rackets" use their wits, "front" and talking ability, and these are regarded by the professional thieves as belonging to the profession.[1]

The inference, as I see it, is that violent crimes, for example those involving the threat or use of violence by way of weapons are thought to require little or no ability to manipulate people. Since the mechanical skills, besides the ability to use a gun, also appear to be minimal, the robber appears to share neither the social skills of the con artist, nor the technical skills of the burglar.

My subjects recognized that some lines demand greater ability in conning the public (obviously, for example, con artists) and that some lines involve no contact with the public at all. Among the latter, however, are some lines, such as burglar-alarm experts who, although not in face-to-face contact with the public, speak of their work in terms of their ability to outsmart the public. The same is true of safecrackers, who violate the ultimate symbols of financial security. Therefore, although the manual aspect of the above lines varies (the safecracker doing much more purely physical labor), each is perceived as an intellectual rather than a physical conquest.[2]

In this chapter on overt crime, it is my purpose to analyse the accounts given by armed robbers, with a view to discovering the assumptions on which the robber proceeds and the skills used in the action.

Just as safecracking was used to illustrate various dimensions of burglary, so group bank robbery will be used here to illustrate facets

---

1. Sutherland, *The Professional Thief*, p. 198.
2. There are exceptions to this, and examples of snobbishness can be documented. For example, no. 35, who was a burglar, recalled his difficulty in opening his first safe. I asked why he had not sought advice from an experienced safecracker. "I wasn't that much interested in it," he said. "Actually, I just rate a safecracker, even the best, only as a laborer." (no. 35)

of robbery. This choice is partly arbitrary, for similar basic patterns can be seen in general armed robbery as well. To focus on bank robbery, however, provides a useful contrast with our previous discussion of safecracking, which is also used to extract money from banks. My subjects frequently suggested that the increasing difficulty of burglarizing a bank is the cause for the rise in bank robberies.

In terms of organization, robbery may involve a highly organized group of persons working as a team; on the other hand, it may be a loose, temporary liaison between several persons, or it may take the form of a lone gunman doing a stick-up. The victims may also vary, from banking institutions to the corner grocer or a lone pedestrian. As indicated later in this chapter under "Procedural Variations," bank robbery may take various forms.

My choice of group bank robbery enables us to look both at the interaction between the group and the bank employees, and at the sociological processes within the group itself. The group formation, the testing of loyalties, and the allocation of responsibilities will be dealt with later under the more general topic of teaching and learning criminal skills. In this chapter, we will look at the act of group robbery itself, so that the technical, organizational, and social skills involved may be documented and described before we ask how they are learned and transmitted.

B. PRE-EVENT PLANNING

If the group is a loose, temporary liaison initiated by a transient robber, the choice of partners will be made at least partly on the basis of the skills required for a particular job. If the group is a coalition of some duration, various responsibilities will be understood and fulfilled by members prior to the event itself. Legal, medical, and financial arrangements may or may not form a part of an individual's prerobbery preparation, depending on his experience and ability to pay.

THE ONLY TOOLS YOU BASICALLY NEED THEN ARE MASKS AND GUNS? Oh no. Definitely, you need more than that. Now this is where organization is the big thing. You see, well—first of all you've got—well, I was shot. Well, I'm shot, see? Now just supposing I'd have got away, where am I going to go? St. Paul's Hospital? Am I gonna go to St. Mary's Hospital? General Hospital? Oh no—I've gotta have a doctor.

You've gotta, so therefore you've gotta have a doctor. You've gotta take care of all these things. You just don't—you've gotta have, in case you go to jail, you've gotta have a lawyer. You've gotta have all these things taken care of long before you go into planning a bank job. Well, where would I have gone if I'd have got shot? Well, I couldn't have stayed in a hotel room, bleeding like a sieve. Right away, if I'd have got out, I'd have just phoned my doctor so and so, and said, "I'm here, get up here right away!" You see, you've gotta pay them off, you see. There's lots of them in Western City. Same also if I'd have got caught, I would have needed a lawyer right away, quick. Things like that. You've got to take care of all these things. WHAT ABOUT BAIL MONEY? Oh, I had that all taken care of. Bail money was taken care of. (no. 7)

It may be for reasons such as these that organized criminals tend to operate within specific areas, despite the fact that such operation draws "heat" on them. The transient criminals enjoy anonymity, but must choose partners from among relative strangers, and sacrifice the insurance provided by arrangements with doctors, lawyers, and bondsmen.

The bank will have been cased beforehand by the one who initiated the robbery. He may or may not have consulted with a partner (before the casing) as to the feasibility of the job. In cases of transient, two-, or three-man groups, casing may be done by all members of the group as they drive leisurely down the streets. In all cases of bank robbery related to me, no member of the group was entirely "cold" (for example, had not as much as seen the bank to be done). The general procedure is for the one who initiated the job to case the place, decide on a suitable time, and then take his partners with him on a dry run the day before the hold-up.

OKAY. LET'S SAY IT'S THE DAY BEFORE—THE DAY BEFORE YOU WANT TO DO THIS. WHAT DO YOU HAVE TO DO THE DAY BEFORE? Well, we usually get our car the night before, and we—well, we naturally check over our weapons. We go through the dry run so to speak, you know. The best exit out. DO YOU DO THAT WITH YOUR OWN CAR? Oh yes. DO YOU MAKE ANY DRAWING AT THAT STAGE? No. BUT YOU'RE ALL TOGETHER AT THIS TIME, RIGHT? Right.

DO YOU SPEND THE NIGHT TOGETHER? We have at times, yeh. But not all the time, not all the time. We—usually, if we're gonna meet in the morning we just sort of casually saunter into a coffee shop, just like the working stiff, you know. Saunter in and have a cup of coffee.

And before you know it there's three of us there and we have our coffee and then we saunter out.

AND YOUR CAR IS READY TO GO? Yeh, that's right—it's all been taken care of. WHEN DID YOU GET THIS CAR? The night before. AND IT'S A STOLEN CAR? [3] That's right. SUPPOSE THE COPS ARE LOOKING FOR THAT CAR BY THAT TIME? That's very unlikely, because we have the plates and that all doctored up.

AT WHAT POINT DO YOU DECIDE WHO DOES WHAT? Well, it's pretty well understood; like you always have one who makes the suggestion, "Let's rob a bank." So, naturally, if you're going to rob a bank, you make the suggestion, you're the one who's going to lay the groundwork for it. So they—well, they just more or less accept you as the leader. (no. 7)

Bank robbers rely heavily on the architectural uniformity of banks. Banks are frequently located on street corners, and this is convenient for getaways. Glass doors permit the robber-doorman to see who is coming in, whereas, as a robber noted, the persons coming in have more difficulty seeing through the glass because of light reflection. The present trend toward low counters, possibly motivated by the bank officials' desire for a more personal and less prison-like atmosphere, is looked upon favorably by bank robbers:

WHAT ABOUT THE HEIGHT OF THE COUNTER? IS THIS A FACTOR? Well, sometimes you see, you might have to jump the counter. Well, if you get some of these real high counters, well—they're tough to get over. Well, you lose a few seconds by getting over the counters, and some of these banks, like, they have these gates like, with—well, you can't reach over and open them because the catch is too far down, so therefore you've got to jump over this counter, you see. The lower the counter, the better I like it. You just hop over the—and hop back, and also you can see just exactly what the man is doing with his hands at all times. (no. 7)

Just as architectural uniformity is assumed, so the presence of mechanical alarm systems is assumed. The use of hidden TV cameras and other devices (the presence of which are advertised with warning stickers) are not a deterrent to the experienced bank rob-

3. Later no. 7 stated:

You never steal your own car—you have somebody do it for you, and pay them off. There's no use incriminating yourself in a car theft, when you're gonna pull a bank job. Therefore, it's worth to you to give some fellow a hundred dollars to get you a car. What's a hundred dollars of the bank's money? Nothing! (no. 7)

ber because he will be "covered" (wearing a mask) anyway, and so he cares little whether he is seen only by bank personnel on the scene or by others via TV. Since the presence of alarm systems is taken for granted, they are neither "cased" nor the object of special attention. The robber assumes they are in working order and that they have gone off the moment he enters the bank.

Although these purely mechanical factors are assumed constant, other factors vary and may affect the difficulty of doing a bank. Some of these may be assessed beforehand. The disposition of the manager is inferred by his apparent age. Those robbers who prefer to deal with as few employees as possible may make daily observations as to the most opportune time. No attention is paid to the number of customers in a bank, except insofar as this indicates the probable number who may wish to enter the bank during the robbery. Persons wishing to enter at this time are much more of a risk to the robber than those already inside. The danger lies in the customer noting that something is wrong before he, or she has entirely entered. Such a customer cannot be prevented from leaving at that point, and becomes the first "alarm." When this happens, the doorman will call his men out immediately.

The safecracker who wants to do a bankjob assumes the presence of money at all times. Primarily, he must consider the *technical* availability, which involves the architecture of a building permitting an "in," the make of the safe, and so forth. The bank robber, on the other hand, must consider the *immediate* availability of money. Unless he is planning a rural robbery, during which he will have time to rob the vault as well as the teller's tills, the bank robber expects to take only what is in the tills.[4] He assumes that the amount carried in tills varies according to day of the week, time of day, and paydays.

The following outline was presented by no. 41:

> The time—on a Monday, if possible. On a Friday, people withdraw for the weekend: Only got two thousand, six hundred dollars on a Friday from three cashiers. Business deposits on Monday—each cashier will have no more than five thousand dollars—some under the box, some above. Businesses need change for the weekend; they don't want to deposit till Monday. On Saturday banks are closed. Businesses may

4. Larger banks, with more tills, are preferred because of their greater cash potential.

make a night deposit—if so, that deposit will also be counted on Monday morning. (no. 41)

The bank robber may plan his robbery on the basis of inferences made from the location of the bank:

> If a bank is near factories, you can be sure it will carry a lot of cash on paydays, which as a rule are on Friday. (no. 39)

Given a suitable commercial context, the thief may wish to assess more specifically the economic potential, particularly with reference to its temporal fluctuations:

> So you see, there's quite a few mills around here, so I sat down and bought some beers for a couple of guys who work in mills, and just in conversation, you know, kind of—the conversation got around to working in these mills and that, and I mentioned that I knew a guy who worked at the mill and who could—and the guy owed me some money and I asked them when—when does this group get paid. I'd like to collect. I'd like to catch him on a day he gets paid. So they told me. So I figured, well, a lot of these guys cash their cheques here and more do on Thursdays than on Fridays, so sure enough I went down the next—the following week on Thursday, and sure enough, and they came around like a couple of trained rats. So I said, the money's there all right—I'll get it here. (no. 2)

While interviewing an urban bank robber I had little success in having him respond to the question, "What time of day is the best time to hit a bank?" He finally responded by saying, "Well, you can't tell, you see—you may not be able to find a parking spot." He noted that sometimes robbers are obliged to cruise around the block repeatedly before a suitable parking spot materializes. The urban bank robber can neither double-park nor park some distance from the bank. The problem of parking, which may be only an annoyance to the shopper, is a vital consideration to the bank robbers. Furthermore, banks, in order to draw customers by providing parking space, also draw unwanted "customers."

The urban parking consideration makes further planning difficult. Knowledge of police patrol must be synchronized with uncertain parking opportunities, which vary within the urban setting. One robber pointed out that parking is seldom a problem in the suburbs. In those instances where parking violations are anticipated, the robber follows what he considers to be "normal" parking violations, that is, violations that will not attract attention. Just as persons in law enforcement offices construct concepts of the "normal" or "typical" crime, so it is assumed by the robber that the layman distinguishes between routine parking violations and atypical ones:

SUPPOSE YOU CAN'T FIND A PARKING SPOT? Oh, we double-park. You see, in these small towns, especially country towns, you see, we're driving a pickup truck; if people see a truck double-parked, motor running, they think it's a farmer who's gone into the bank for a minute—so it takes away all suspicion. We make sure it's an old truck, but with a fairly good motor in it. (no. 8)

C. PROCEDURAL VARIATIONS

Although the detailed differences that make every robbery unique cannot be dealt with here, I will indicate how some situational contingencies and individual preferences shape the procedures employed. The emphasis, however, will be upon those variations necessitated by social, geographical, and other structural factors.

Our procedure here will be to present a first-hand account, recorded verbatim, of a small-town bank robbery, its most distinctive feature being that it is rural. Its ruralism distinguishes it from an urban robbery in terms of speed required, parking opportunities available, and risk of police intervention.

Example

The way we do in the provincial field when I hit that town, we usually hit them that have somewhere in the neighborhood of five thousand population. They have generally one police that police the whole town, you know. So we're not afraid of this guy—he's nothing. We drive the car, and two of us would be behind the seat and with the door open, the hoods on, the guns ready. The driver would start to slow down when he comes to the bank and call "three, two, one." And then we open the door and we run as fast as we can. Into that bank. Because whoever comes in first, he's got ten dollars more than the rest of us got, you know. It's just to—yeh, just to give us an urge, you know. IS THAT RIGHT? Yeh. And the first guy that enters the bank goes over the counter. The second guy which follows him, which is very fast, goes for the manager's office. The third guy stays by the door.[5] And the driver comes in last.[6] NOW, WHAT DOES HE DO WITH THE

5. The work positions are determined by the central concern of the operation, namely speed. All persons must be capable of performing equally well in different positions; however, the door-man has the most dangerous position, requiring the greatest degree and variety of skills. The fact that, in this group, the door-man

CAR? The car—the doors are open, and it stays like that. Now, I look at the people in the street—I watch them so that nobody will come near the car.

IS IT PARKED WHERE ALL THE OTHER CARS ARE? No, no. Parking—we don't care about parking, whether or not. We drive right in front of the bank where the door is the closest to it, even if it's on the sidewalk, and there's a thing that goes on the sidewalk. And if there's one there we go right on the sidewalk. Period! Because we figure that as soon as we open the door of the car, we assume that the alarm is going off right there.

And we act accordingly. So we are tense right there, you know. We are full of tension. And once the action starts, you got no tension any more.[7] You know, you're so busy watching; looking there, watching there—"On the floor there!" Watching that car pass by, you know. "Get the fuck out of there!" And things like that, you know. You're not afraid anymore. But I'm afraid before I go into the bank though. The moment I sit on that back seat or I'm driving that car coming to the bank, I'm looking all over the place and I'm full of tension. I'm ready to bunch up. If somebody would say, "boo!" behind me, you know, I'd go right through that roof!

WHAT ABOUT THE DRIVER—IS HE WEARING A HOOD? Everything.

WELL, AREN'T YOU BEING NOTICED THEN, BY PEOPLE ON THE STREET? It's funny. It's funny how people—I've noticed that. It's been noted too —that most of—I'll tell you more than that—on three banks we walked into the bank, we got out, and the people were walking by, and they thought it was Halloween or something phony.[8] They didn't

---

would be the first to enter and temporarily take up a different position is unusual. It may be accounted for by the fact that all members of this group are highly experienced. The more common pattern, I was told, is better expressed by no. 7:

> I usually go in last. If I'm the leader I go in last. Now this is my own—some guys may do it differently. But I go in last and I come out last. (no. 7)

6. The role of the driver varies with the rural-urban factor. In an urban bank robbery, the driver would likely remain in the car and have the car already moving as the partners return and jump inside. He will try to look inconspicuous, perhaps with a newspaper in his hand. He is responsible for watching for opposition, either civilian or police. Besides having driving ability, he must be absolutely reliable. He is expected to remain on the scene should the police arrive.

7. The lack of tension while on the job is in contrast to the anxiety of the employees—an anxiety induced and deliberately aggravated by the robbers. It must also be viewed as a necessary skill—the situation, in which mistakes may mean death, demands quick, rational decisions.

8. This illustrates how the public is accustomed to some deviation from the normal in society, and how the robber can take advantage of this.

know it was something real happening. You know, they realize when people start to scream, "Holdup, bandit!" and things like that. Then they say, "Oh, my god—how close I was to that guy!" You know.

SO, YOU'RE NOT GOING TO BE BOTHERED ABOUT A PARK SPOT? Oh no, not in a provincial. In the city you would have to. You know, because then the police are patrolling the street all the time, yeh. You got to park at the proper place or otherwise you are going to have opposition right there and then. WELL, WELL.

NOW, LET'S STAY WITH THE SEQUENCE HERE. YOU GENERALLY TRAVEL IN TWO CARS? Two cars, yes. Two stolen cars. Like, my car and my partner's car. Two guys per car, you see, and the stolen car; we drive them two days before. They're parked there and they're there, and we drive back with our own car. Because these are the cars that we're going to go through the roadblock with, and the two stolen cars, they are going to be dumped out or sometimes we reverse the tank and we set fire to it or sometimes we don't even bother with that.

WELL, LET'S SEE NOW. YOU'RE TWO MEN TO THE CAR WHEN YOU DRIVE INTO THE TOWN HERE. And you know—suppose the bank is here and the street is here, and there's a connecting street here. Now, we stop the first car here. We got hoods on. But as you stop here the two guys goes out and I'm right in front. They just jump in and we keep going. And then we come back and if everything goes good, everything goes good here we don't worry about that car—we leave it there. We just keep going. Because this car is completely useless to us anymore. This car is just put there in case of emergency. I SEE.

Diagram:

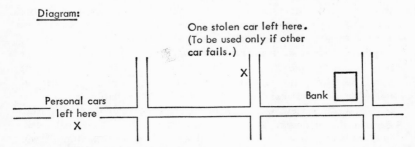

AND YOU SAY THAT THERE'S NO SET ORDER AS TO WHO GETS IN THE BANK FIRST? No. The one who runs fastest is the one who goes in. I stay at the door, but suppose now I run faster than my partner—I go in. The first thing I do—I'll jump over the counter,[9] you know.

---

9. Even the most important position is temporarily left vacant in the interest of speed. It is most important that the tellers are moved away from their counters and alarm buttons as quickly as possible.

I give the order "On the floor!" and then everybody goes on the floor, and I'll smash somebody—the one who is closest to me. I'm going to have to smash him in the face. "On the floor, in the corner!" [10] Now, by that time, by the time I say that, my three other partners are in. The one is already going into the office and I backstep right to the door, and then I take my position. And now I watch the car outside. I watch the employees. If someone gets up, or something like that. And I watch the people which are on this side of the counter also.[11]

NOW, IF YOUR BANK IS BUILT LIKE THIS,[12] LIKE MANY OF THEM ARE,

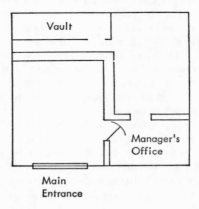

Main
Entrance

WITH THE DOOR HERE, AND THE BANKING COUNTER, AND THIS IS THE MANAGER'S OFFICE—YOU'VE GOT TO JUMP OVER THAT COUNTER. THERE'S A DOOR HERE AND A DOOR THERE. IF YOU MUST JUMP OVER THIS WAY, HOW DO YOU MANAGE THIS FELLOW IN THE FRONT? I don't worry about him. If I'm the one that comes in the bank first, I don't worry about him. I just jump in the corner here, on top here, and the door will likely be closed anyway, eh? And there will probably be someone having an interview with this manager. I don't bother with him. Because the manager, also—they know about that. They still freeze in their office, just thinking, "Is that a joke, or something?" you know. And the—by the time he starts to react, like it takes only maybe three seconds, the whole sequence there. I give a yell, "All on the

10. When recalling another robbery, no. 28 elaborated further on the psychology of this initial violence. See discussion p. 109.
11. The robber is continuously assessing the probable meaning of his victims' movements.
12. Diagram of bank as sketched by no. 28.

floor!" and then by the time I give my yell people look at me—they are kind of undecided and I'll smash the first guy and back I go, because my partner is on the side of the counter and one is busting the door open and "Out you go!" and there you are, you know. And I'm back at the door here—I take my position.

OKAY, YOU'RE BACK HERE. NOW, TWO FELLOWS, NO, THREE . . . ? Three. We usually work four. Now, one guy goes in here—he gets everything in there. One will go to the toilet, or wherever, the washroom or the employees washroom—sometimes they are downstairs, you know. He goes down there and he cleans everything out there, and the third one . . . WHAT DOES HE DO DOWN THERE? Well, he gathers all the people—there may be—he bursts—sometimes he got guys with their pants halfway down—grabs the guy, "Up you go!" Yeh, no choice. You can't say, "Well, have your crap and please come up," you know.

WHY DON'T YOU JUST HAVE HIM STAY THERE AND JUST BE SURE NONE OF THEM LEAVE? Oh, well, we can't because you see, this guy here, by the time he stays down there all the time, suppose actions start here at the door—somebody starts popping shot in through that window—I want to—I want this guy to be up there pretty fast, you know. And he leaves that guy down there, you know—how do I know that he hasn't got a gun concealed in there somewhere down there? He'll bring them up and push them all up in one corner. Now we know that all the people are in one corner—they cannot be of any harm to us. If there happened to be a police officer in the bunch, I'm watching that guy there all the time. If a guy goes and makes a move there, he got his hands on his head you know. And if he makes a move I got time to react to him, and I say, "What are you doing there?" And if I got a suspicion it may be a police officer I may just knock him off, you know—give him a good blow in the head and knock him cold, or things like that. But you cannot have dispersion in the bank. If the guy is down near here, and suddenly action occur, and this guy wants to know what's going on, and so you have to leave this guy here and run upstairs.

NOW, BANKS ARE MOSTLY BUILT THE SAME WAY, I GUESS. Right. BUT SOMETIMES THEY ARE A LITTLE DIFFERENT. DO YOU, BEFORE YOU COME THERE THAT DAY, GO THROUGH THAT BANK AND SEE WHERE THE WASHROOM IS, AND WHERE THIS IS AND WHERE THAT IS? No. Sometime we do that but very often not, because I don't want to be identified after. OH, I SEE. But sometime we know—you see, the provincial banks in ———, for example. They build in a certain manner. A National Bank maybe in a slightly different manner, but it's so close that after you have done maybe two or three banks it comes automatic. Just two or three. It's reflex action. You get in and you see that the

manager's office—you don't have to worry, is the—is this the assistant?
Yes it is—it's the manager's office. You burst the door open and see
what's there and push them out. Period! And you see a door connecting downstairs; well, right away you say—this is a bank that I'm
sure, that must be the toilet in there, you know. And away out one
goes, you know.

OKAY NOW, ONE GUY IS CLEANING OUT THE BATHROOMS, ONE GUY IS IN
THE MANAGER'S OFFICE, ONE—YOU'RE AT THE DOOR, AND ONE FELLOW IS
SCOOPING UP THE MONEY. Scooping—well, first you make sure that all
the people are in the corner. Take a fast look into the vault, and then
he scoops the cash. Then, by that time the two other guys will enter
the vault with the manager, and we have—we try to have the first
safe opened.

There's always a big safe—there's four tellers in that bank. The
association—insurance association, will not cover more than five thousand dollars, for example, in teller's, [till] where they call "risky
area," right? So now they have the first door in the safe and there's
four small other safes. You know, a case like that. Now, you call,
"first teller." First teller comes in and opens her safe. Now, anything
in excess of her money she puts in that safe until four o'clock and
then she counts it. Now, you scoop that money in, and you open them
four safes.[13] We never have time to go for the treasury,[14] which is
another safe—that sits way at the—most of the time at the end of the
vault.[15] And this big safe is what they call the "treasury." All the
money, rolling money, you know, of the bank is there. So we get them
four as fast as we can.

NOW, THOSE FOUR HAVE TO BE OPENED BY THE TELLERS? Yeh—we call
them "first teller, second teller, third, and fourth." SO, THEY'VE GOT
TO COME AND OPEN THESE? Yes. Well, we get the manager to call them.
You know, we grab the manager by the head, and you know, "Come
on, move!" "Call the first teller, you cocksucker!" And he calls them
in, Mrs. so-and-so, and we're ready to go. And they are all pretty
excited and they don't like the pressure of sharp commands like that,
and dirty language—we use very often too, you know. To upset them
as much as possible we can. Don't let them think—we don't want

13. Note the robber's above-average knowledge of banking procedures.
14. Although the rural bank robber has not the time to get all the money
kept in the bank, he does attempt access to considerably more than his urban
counterpart. Urban robbers, who spend less than two minutes in a bank, will
not ask for any of the money in the vault, but must be content with till money.
(That is, unless they have planned for special monies, such as safety deposit
monies—to be discussed later.)
15. Uniform architecture, undoubtedly an economic consideration for banks,
is of advantage to the bank robber as well.

region?" "Well, we were fishing in that region. You know, we felt like going for an outdoor—going, you know—going in a field for a—having a—enjoy ourself!" We had a case of beer in the car—we had fishing rods and things like that, nature—a compass, you know—a compass and things like that, to go into the bush. So they—we got something to justify our being in that region, for the lawyer. In case it goes to court. That's the main thing. And then we go through the road block.

NOW, I WOULD IMAGINE THESE FELLOWS AT THE ROAD BLOCK WOULD FAIRLY SOON KNOW WHOM TO LOOK FOR. Yes, they do, but then, what can they do? What can they do? The police officers, you know him, let's say you recognize me—well, I say, "How are you doing?" "Well! How are you doing! You bastard! You just been there, eh?" "Well, gee, I don't know anything—I just come from the creek there." "Is that a fact? Let's search the fuckin' car first, right?" "Okay, I'll help you— I'll help you search my car—you want me to strip right here—I'll strip with pleasure." You know, the more they search me the better you give me a beef in case I go to court. Because my lawyer will question you, and as soon as you say that you've searched this person so thoroughly that you couldn't barely pass a dollar bill there, then home-free I am.

AND HE CAN'T ARREST YOU, IF HE HASN'T ANYTHING ON YOU? Well, he could possibly say, "Well, okay, I'll bring you in for, say what—24 hours." Well, I don't care about that. I'll go twenty-four hours anytime for five thousand dollars—you know that part.

WHAT WOULD YOUR NORMAL TAKE BE IN A BANK LIKE THAT—A SMALL PLACE? Yeh—they never have reached more than twenty or twenty-five thousand at the most. That's the very most. SO THAT GIVES YOU FOR FOUR PEOPLE . . . ? That's about five thousand each. Well, usually we average about three thousand each. THREE THOUSAND EACH.

OKAY. NOW, HOW SOON DO YOU COME BACK FOR THE MONEY IN THE BUSH? We usually come back somewhere between four and seven days. So, because they're smart, them guys too—they know we plant the money. I mean, they watch us. (no. 28)

D. DIMENSIONS OF VICTIM MANAGEMENT

The skills required for crimes involving the avoidance of the victim are signficantly different from the skills required for crimes involving victim confrontation. Surreptitious crimes tend to revolve around mechanical competences, whereas crimes involving victim confrontation revolve around victim management. The term "management" is chosen to differentiate this process from what might be termed "victim manipulation," as in confidence games.[21]

My focus on victim management is not intended to obscure other differences, nor to suggest that criminals develop mechanical or social skills to the exclusion of the other; I have earlier pointed out that thieves may engage in both types of crimes. The focus arises, instead, from the distinctions made by the criminals themselves, and from inherent differences in mechanical versus social skills.

1. Surprise and Vulnerability

The bank robber relies on surprise to bring about momentary mental and physical paralysis of bank employees:

> The door would fly right open and the people inside, they freeze! (no. 28)

Such paralysis is crucially important to the bank robber: it allows him quickly to take up his position in the building; further, he hopes to be able to back all cashiers away from their counter before they have had a chance to regain enough composure to push an alarm button.

Criminals believe that bank employees' susceptibility to surprise and their consequent vulnerability varies with the time of day and the day of week. A bank robber insisted mornings are the best time:

> OKAY. NOW WHAT TIME OF DAY? Always in the morning. Catch them by surprise. They've still got sleep in their eyes and sort of hung over if they drink. Catch them by surprise. About ten o'clock. (no. 7)

A bank robber who preferred Monday mornings, said:

> On Monday, everybody's asleep; not asleep, but not going anywhere. People are dull. On Monday, people are not on the street in the morning—people are either asleep or at work. (no. 41)

The criminal is also aware that his surprised victim is not in a position to react efficiently, even if he should try to. A burglar involved in the "live prowl" stated:

> WERE YOU PREPARED IN ANY SENSE IN THE EVENT OF BEING CAUGHT? Well, you don't think of that. 'Course I always made sure, like you

---

21. Under some conditions victim manipulation develops into a situation of victim management. Erving Goffman, "On Cooling the Mark Out," *Psychiatry* 15, no. 4 (November 1952).

say, that there were ways out. 'Cause I never thought of being cornered by anyone there, because most people when they wake up, they're stunned, you know, anyhow; they're not that wide awake, so you're wide awake, you know. You're going to get out of the place. (no. 21)

This resembles the bank robber's inducement of near hysteria in order to create an imbalance in the degree of rationality the robber and the victims are respectively capable of.

In addition, the victim is not equipped with the skills required to reverse his position of weakness, even if he should recover from his surprise:

> But in the long run, your chances of ever using a gun on a professional thief are very small—you're better off without a gun—you'll probably get your head shot off because he's doing something he does every day and you're doing something you've never done before.[22]

2. *Establishing Authority and Managing Tension*

The initial moment of surprise and shock is the first step in establishing a robber-victim relationship. During this time, the entire group may be herded into one corner of the bank, or ordered to lie prostrate on the floor. In either case, the posture and physical location of the victims are such as to enhance the robber's control over them.

Once having established control, some robbers encourage the return of rational thought to the victim, while others prefer to extend the state of shock until the robbery is completed. In either case, the particular style adopted seems to be a matter of personal preference rather than a choice based on features of the specific robbery itself. Through experience, robbers adopt a style they find effective in managing the victim. The robber quoted next seeks to maintain victim management by continuing the state of shock in his victims.

> . . . the door would fly right open and the people inside, they freeze. You know, when there's a big smash around everyone they freeze on the spot and look around, whether it's a joke or not. And you see them guys, you know; and they have hoods on their heads, and the gun, you know. And then there's one command—"Hit the ground!" you know —"Hit the dirt!"—I don't know how to say that—"Hit the floor—

22. Martin, *My Life in Crime*, p. 69.

bunch of dogs!," you know. That's the way we say that: "Fuckin' dog, hit the floor, or we kill each and every one of you!," you know. So they are froze there—their reaction is one of very extreme fear and they drop on the floor and sometime we select the strongest person— the manager especially or another teller which is very big—a six footer, or something like that, you know. And we won't say a word, we just walk up to him and smash him right across the face, you know, and we get him down. And once he's down the people, the girls especially, they look at him and they say, "My God—big Mike, he's been smashed down like that—I'd better lay down too, and stay quiet." You know—it's sort of like psychology, to obey us immediately, every- body will follow the leader. The manager is the leader, and I see you go down—Jesus Christ, I'm going to follow you—I'm going down too, you know! (no. 28)

Another bank robber, in contrast, is anxious to avoid hysteria:

That's how I used to operate. I'd stand right there and the manager and the whole works at bay. I might have them lay down on the floor, 'cause you couldn't just have them standing there with their hands up, because it's too noticeable. You just walk in, and anyone you think is going to panic, well you just talk real quiet to them and you say, "Don't panic and everything will be all right; just take it easy and there'll be no trouble, see?"

DID YOU USE TO FIRE ANY SHOTS INTO THE CEILING OR ANYTHING LIKE THAT? No—I used to talk very softly—I'd talk very softly, very quietly, and I'd never raise my voice. I always figure that if you holler and show panic, it would make the people panicky. If you just walk in quietly, just like you're transacting ordinary business, it kinda reassures the people that you know exactly what you're doing, and that you mean them no harm. But if you go in there hustling and bustling and firing and shooting, you're going to have people start to scream, and everything else. And it's pretty hard to hold back people screaming no matter what pressure they're under.

BUT ISN'T THERE THE PROBLEM THAT IF YOU SPEAK SOFTLY THERE MAY BE SOMEONE AT THE BACK AT AN ADDING MACHINE . . . ? Oh well, they automatically know. You don't speak that softly. You know, when we walk in we say, "This is a holdup!" and they automatically hear you. But then after that you just sort of—no worry, no rush. It's just a mat- ter of routine—load up the money, and your shopping bags and go out. Oh, we make sure that everybody hears you, that's for sure. We don't just walk in there and say, "Well, this is a holdup, hand over the money." We give a good bellow when we walk in.[23] (no. 7)

23. This is similar to the approach used by the robber described in "The Heist . . ." by DeBaum. On page 74, he states:

Bank robbers emphasize self-confidence as the key to successful bank robbery. They directly relate self-confidence to the ability to control people who are under stress. The manner in which this confidence is communicated is secondary, but it is essential that it be communicated.

Number 45 stressed the importance of making it clear to those in the bank that his group "meant business":[24]

> They can tell by the sound of your voice, by what you say and how you go about things, whether or not you mean business. If you're shaky, they'll know.[25] (no. 45)

The role of "voice" in establishing authority and in managing tension is considered critical to bank robbery, and to armed robbery in general. The methods used are visual (masks, hoods), auditory (vocal commands), and physical.

> SO WHAT WOULD YOU SAY ARE THE DANGERS IN THIS KIND OF AN OPERATION? Uh—well, panic on the part of the store owner. WHAT FORMS CAN THAT TAKE? Uh—I've experienced a man literally freezing —couldn't speak. He just pointed to show where the money was. SO THAT DIDN'T CAUSE YOU MUCH TROUBLE? No, no. But on occasion I've had women scream. WHAT DO YOU DO IN THAT CASE? Well, on a couple of occasions I've just belted them on the side of the head with the pistol. KNOCK THEM OUT OR WHAT? No. SO THAT'S ONE WAY OF DEALING WITH WOMEN WHO SCREAM? Or slap them in the face with the fist. The man I worked with was well over six feet and a very powerful built man with a deep resonant voice, and I saw him just with a loud voice, and with the tone of his voice, he would bring people out of a shock state.
>
> IS THE MANNER IN WHICH YOU SPEAK VERY IMPORTANT? Very much so —yeh—you have to be positive at all times. DID YOU EVER HAVE ANY TROUBLE, LET'S SAY, WITH A WOMAN WHO WOULDN'T COOPERATE? I didn't, no. (no. 27)

> So far as may be, the mob are calm and polite on the job. "Cowboying" or the wild brandishing of pistols and shouting of orders in all directions is frowned upon; fear has made more heroes than courage ever has.

DeBaum pays detailed attention to some aspects of victim management in armed bank robbery. [Everett DeBaum, "The Heist: The Theory and Practice of Armed Robbery," *Harpers* 200 (February 1950): 69–77.]

24. This raises the question of why bank personnel find it difficult to accept the reality of a robbery.

25. Number 45 was described to me by other criminals as "very good in banks," and as having a "very good voice for banks."

Another example regarding the use of language:

> Now, her mother and brother they were at the back of the bank, you know, of the house, and they heard that, because, you know, my talking during a bank holdup is very different from the talking we have now—it's full of tension and very commanding, you know. In order to impress the people as much as we possibly can. (no. 28)

What bank robbers seem to be describing has certain similarities with what Max Weber has defined as "charisma." Robbers refer to these qualities, such as voice and physical build, as inherent, rather than as techniques that might be learned. It is more difficult, however, to delineate the various dimensions of what robbers refer to as "confidence." Some clues have been provided; in crime, as elsewhere, success breeds success:

> AND YOU WERE PRETTY SURE THAT YOU COULD KEEP THIS UP WITHOUT TROUBLE? Oh yes, definitely—most of the guys that I've met, and I've met a tremendous amount of criminals, you know, that were involved in a bank robbery, and we feel very confident; as a matter of fact, anyone who does two banks and he succeeds going all through and he has no police suspicion on him, he becomes over confident, you know. You say, "Well, now I'm a master criminal and I know how to do it. They didn't catch me, they're not aware that I'm working on it, and everything goes smoothly—it will work forever like that." You know, you get confident like that. (no. 28)

Number 28 points out that confidence can be dangerous, encouraging false notions of immunity from danger. Yet it appears to be precisely this confidence that facilitates successful robbery. In a sense, the robber cannot afford to consider possible or even probable consequences of his action, lest such considerations deprive him of the confidence needed to complete the task successfully.

Number 40 noted that, objectively and rationally, the probability of a prison sentence ought to deter the criminal. He added, however, that the criminal cannot afford to consider these matters, particularly just before a holdup, because he will lose his confidence. At that stage, it is rational *not* to consider failure, since by so doing you will bring it upon yourself all the more surely.

Although the degree of tension felt by a robber appears to vary from person to person, it is clear that he must manage his own tension besides his victims'. Number 28 said he is very tense before a holdup, whereas to no. 7 it was just "like getting up and having a shave and having coffee and going to work."

The ability to manage one's own tension affects work roles. It is generally agreed that it is essential for the door-man to be armed but that the other accomplices can do without weapons. Only those who have demonstrated their ability to control themselves will be given guns:

> The man with experience carries the gun; the reason he carries the gun is that he won't pull the trigger right away. Everybody is nervous; if a guy is too nervous you don't give him a gun—it's too dangerous. (no. 39)

Another stated:

> Getting the money is the easiest job for the least experienced or nervous person. (no. 41)

Experienced criminals may demand that less experienced partners be unarmed, or armed with less effective weapons. An experienced burglar who worked with two less experienced partners insisted they carry knives rather than guns:

> You think twice with a knife. A person going with a gun, if he has to use it, he'll use it right away, whereas a person with a knife, if he can dodge it, he will. Say, for instance, if you saw a guy in the place, instead of panicking and blowing the guy's head right off, with a knife you can move back into the shadow, and you don't panic, you just relax. With a gun you're likely to shoot the guy, with a knife you gotta stab him which means you come in close contact with him to stab him. (no. 10)

Ability to manage their own fears is also requisite for the driver of the holdup car, particularly when it is necessary for the driver to remain in the car during the holdup. His opportunity to leave the scene in relative safety is in stark contrast to the situation of his partners. Whether or not the driver remains in the car appears to be related both to the reliability of the driver and the degree of pressure he is exposed to:

> In the old days, they used to leave the driver of a bank car outside, and most times they'd come out and the car would be gone! Now, you take the driver with you and he's the first one out. DO YOU THINK THAT IS WHY THEY TAKE THE DRIVER WITH THEM? Definitely, no other reason. (no. 15)

Another respondent:

> YOU LEAVE THE MOTOR RUNNING? Yes. WITH NO ONE IN THE CAR?
> That's the way I would do it. Sure, because if something happens and
> this guy panics and takes off with the car—which has happened, but
> not to me. (no. 36)

Experienced bank robbers feel their work is made more difficult,
and the victim's situation more dangerous, by the tendency of the
mass media to depict bank robberies as phony, "toy gun stuff." Robbers feel they are now constrained first of all to convince their victims the event is "not a joke." This may require more brutal action
on their part than they would otherwise need to use. They need to
convince any potential "heroes" among their victims that they cannot be subdued, TV dramas to the contrary.

The establishment of authority is no doubt enhanced by the display and use of weapons. The discussion above is intended to indicate, however, that the gun is only one of various persuasive devices
used by robbers. This is not to deny that the successful use of other
resources such as loud commands and physical violence is possible
only because he has a gun. Nevertheless, much of the robber's activity during a robbery is necessitated only because he does not want to
use his gun. He is, therefore, rightly dismayed at the condescension
of those who fail to appreciate that his techniques revolve around
the nonuse, rather than the use, of guns.

Such condescension is obvious in the statement of a con man serving a sentence for armed robbery:

> He had great pride in his previous achievements as a con man but
> said that anyone could stick a gun in a sucker's belly and get some
> money and that anyone who did this and landed in prison for it
> should feel ashamed.[26]

If guns are carried for purposes of intimidation only, then why
not use toy guns? The answers were unanimous: "It's too dangerous
—you've got nothing to protect yourself with." (no. 39) Such protection may be needed because of police or potential heroes among
robbery victims. Robbers have only contempt for the hero type,
whose action is considered irrational and extremely dangerous.
Whenever the robber meets resistance from his victims and is
forced to shoot, he is almost certainly going to "win," given his ex-

26. Sutherland, *Professional Thief*, p. 42.

perience and advantageous position. Such "winning," however, has serious legal implications. Also, the scuffle will likely disrupt the orderly retrieval of money, forcing him to leave empty-handed. The bank robber does not want trouble—he wants money:

> Well, this is where the public makes an awfully tragic mistake. It's a tragic mistake and I think maybe there would be a lot less people getting shot in holdups if people were just told that the money is there—give it to the man and leave it to the police. And you've seen in the paper time and time again where people have been shot chasing them down the street. Mind you, they may catch the odd one, but they've only got to shoot one man and it's tragic, you know what I mean. And actually I don't want to shoot anybody, but if it's me or you, you're going first, I'll tell you that right now. (no. 7)

Although the robber will hesitate to use his gun on a civilian, confrontation by police is seen as resulting inevitably in a "shoot-out." "Why not put up your hands and surrender when cornered?" I asked. That seemed incomprehensible: "They'd mow you down. They can just say we resisted arrest." (no. 39)

Bank robbers do not anticipate resistance from a single patrolman but are prepared for it should it occur. Such resistance would be interpreted as a stupid "hero act," similar to a civilian's:

> Have you ever heard of a smart detective getting shot? No, the only ones you ever hear of getting shot are some dumb patrolmen. What do you think so-and-so [a detective] would do if he pulled up alongside a car and a guy raised a chopper? [Submachine gun] You think he'd be a hero? No—he's got brains. He'd get away from there as fast as he could. But he'd eventually find out who that was. Where a dumb patrolman hasn't got enough sense to do that.[27]

Police are expected to arrive in a group, or more likely, to be waiting in the bank. The experienced robber, however, does not expect to be apprehended while at work. If he is to have "trouble," he expects it upon arrival at the bank, or after he has left. To meet it upon arrival indicates an information leak, considered by robbers as their most serious uncontrollable contingency.

The successful management of victims during a robbery demands the continuous and correct interpretation of the victim's behavior. As such, it is important the robber understands correctly the non-verbal communication that is going on—a particularly difficult task,

27. Martin, *My Life in Crime*, p. 100.

since the degree of tension encourages abnormal behavior. Robbers pointed out numerous examples of bizarre behavior on the part of the victims. The most common observed in banks took the form of bank customers offering their own valuables to the robbers, presumably to enhance their own chances of survival. On the other hand, some customers will go to great lengths to hide their own wallets, rings, and jewellery. Such actions must be interpreted as a threatening move. When this occurs, the robber may issue a warning, or shoot. One respondent, an experienced robber, said he was in prison now because of an error he had made in this regard:

> The guy wouldn't stop moving—I didn't know what he was doing, so I let him have it. Later, I found out he was just trying to hide something under a rug.

The data and analysis presented in this chapter enable us to compare and contrast the work of the safecracker with that of the armed robber. They share those concerns generated by the illegality of their work. Both must avoid apprehension and conviction, and reduce the risk of such by way of insurances such as arrangements with friends, bondsmen, and lawyers. Both share certain skills needed for casing, though the specific nature and application of these skills differ, as will be shown in Chapter 6. Despite the above similarities, the contrasts in specific work patterns are striking. The behavior of an armed robber at work is very different from that of a safecracker. Since an armed robber manages people in crisis, and the safecracker uses mechanical skills, an analogy between a psychiatrist and a mechanic may be appropriate. The mere fact that both of the latter work roles are legal, does not blind us to their important differences. In the study of crime, however, we have permitted the fact of its illegality to obscure significant behavioral differences.

Having delineated the various skills and procedures appropriate to both surreptitious and overt crimes, we now turn to the question of how these skills are learned and transmitted. Although learning normally precedes behavior, the reverse chapter sequence used here is necessitated by the fact that it is difficult to appreciate the complexities of the learning process unless the substance of that learning is first understood.

5

LEARNING TECHNICAL SKILLS

A. INTRODUCTION

There are, essentially, two classes of criminal skills. There are, first of all, those that appear to be extensions of the legitimate order, that is, skills available to all members of society. Such skills include the ability to detect when home owners are not home, or to pose as a customer when not really interested in buying. These skills are systematized, sharpened, and refined by the criminal who consciously uses them.

Secondly, some criminals possess skills that are not easily available to the average citizen. Indeed, access to such skills is also differentially distributed among those criminals who seriously desire them. Such skills include the mechanical procedures necessary for safeopening, or the organizational know-how necessary for successful bank robbery.

The distinction between the two classes of criminal skills is implied by Sutherland when he speaks of "larceny sense" as an "indefinite body of appreciations" and as distinct from "techniques of theft." [1] The former is "assimilated" gradually, rather than learned through instruction or experience as is the latter. As I indicate in the following chapter, a good deal of what Sutherland terms "larceny sense" has its basis in commonsense interpretations of the so-

1. Sutherland, *The Professional Thief*, p. 214.

117

cial structure. The systematizing of these common-sense assumptions, so as to make them relevant for nonlegitimate purposes, seems to begin during teen-age delinquency. All of the subjects I interviewed began their criminal behavior during adolescence. This is not to suggest that delinquency causes later crime, but simply to suggest that a person does not enter crime as an adult after a period of legitimate life-style—early delinquency does seem to be a prerequisite for the adult criminal career.

Cloward, in response to Merton's theory of anomie, has indicated that access to the illegitimate (as to the legitimate) is not evenly distributed.[2] It may be that early delinquency constitutes one of the conditions for access to the adult criminal career.

Early delinquency provides a basic education in rudimentary skills appropriate to the illegitimate life-style. It may well be that, at the time when the young person is busily engaged in learning the difference between the appropriate and inappropriate, matters of etiquette, and the role expectations in the legitimate social structure, he is able to see most easily how such arrangements may be manipulated for very different ends.

Early delinquency may also be viewed as an experiment or trial. One's taste, as well as one's ability for the criminal life-style can be assessed, both by oneself and by peers. It makes possible the reformatory experience, which opens the door to association with criminals, and effectively severs the ties with the legitimate order.

The nature of nontechnical skills is discussed in the following chapter. In this chapter, discussion is limited to the acquisition of technical and mechanical skills.

B. THE DELINQUENT STYLE

Experienced criminals relate their early delinquent behavior with a good deal of humor. Their recollections dwell on the aspect of adventure—the humor having to do with what now appears to them to have been a preponderance of daring over ability.

Their early technical skills are described as simple applications of everyday knowledge. A safecracker, now age fifty, recalls the first safe he opened:

2. Cloward, "Illegitimate Means, Anomie, and Deviant Behavior," pp. 164–76.

I had—like we hit a safe in the meantime, you know. When we were just kids; we got the safe open, it was a very cheap safe. We got it open and we had—we had a pretty fair bank roll for kids, you know. About two hundred dollars apiece when we split it up—about two hundred. Why that was just—that was—I just turned fifteen about a week before. We took it (the safe) in one of these stores—a small general store, and it was a cheap safe.

HOW DID YOU MANAGE TO OPEN IT? Well, we used two or three screw drivers, that's how bad the safe was—we kept stepping over, you know, till we got it open. STEPPING OVER—WHAT'S THAT? Well, we started on the corner, you know. And then we drove another one in, you know, and kept stepping till we got it open. (no. 32)

The absence of technical sophistication is evident in the following example of teen-age house burglary:

LET'S LOOK, IN FACT, AT HOW YOU'D GOTTEN AROUND. HOW DID YOU CHOOSE A HOUSE TO ENTER? Well, that's what I say—like for a time I'd walk around. Like let's say in the ———— district. They built that new district there. I'd walk around and I'd see a house with all the lights out. Well, I'd go up and knock at the door. If nobody answered, then I'd know right away. Then, if somebody did answer, well I'd just say, "Does so-and-so live here?" and most people would say, "Well, no, I don't know that person." The majority of times when I did knock I knew nobody was home anyway, because the lights were all out.

SO WHAT DID YOU DO IF NO ONE WAS HOME? Well, I'd go in through the back door; just make a hole through the window and open the door. JUST BREAK THE WINDOW. Yeh, with a rock. DID YOU HAVE TO CARRY ANY TOOLS WITH YOU? No. WHAT TIME OF DAY WOULD YOU DO THIS KIND OF STUFF? Oh, usually in the winter between seven and nine. Six, seven, nine—around there.

OKAY. LET'S SAY YOU'VE KNOCKED ON THE DOOR, NO ONE ANSWERS. YOU GO AROUND THE BACK. YOU BREAK THE WINDOW, OPEN THE DOOR. YOU WALK IN AND IT'S DARK. DO YOU HAVE A LIGHT WITH YOU, OR HOW DO YOU OPERATE? Well, sometimes I used to carry a flashlight. Sometimes I used to turn the light on in the house. I'd go in the bedroom, turn the light on, walk around, and turn it back off. You see, I wasn't there that long; I was just looking for the money, and if I didn't find it I'd leave. . . .

NOW, DURING THIS TIME, WERE YOU ALSO HOLDING DOWN A JOB OF SOME SORT? Yeh. I was working at different jobs—for a month, maybe three months. Then I'd get fired or I'd quit. So then I'd be broke again and then I'd go back to stealing again, 'cause I couldn't get a job right away. (no. 21)

Early B & E's are referred to as "kick-ins"—applying physical force to doors and windows. Such technical "skills" were not learned in any formal sense, though they may have been prompted by social pressure:

> And these guys were kicking joints in and everything; like, from school, and we were getting razzed about being sissies, so we acted, or reacted, I guess, and we got to be pretty tough eggs ourselves during the next, well—in my case, the next forty years, or thirty-five. (no. 32)

Another example, quoting my notes taken during an interview with no. 14:

> Number 14 went to a fair in Regina one summer and ran into one of the guys he had met at reform school. This friend had introduced him to another person—a former boxer. "They were quite the characters." The three of them spent the week in Regina, just talking and fooling around, and one of them came back to Moose Jaw with him. While having coffee in a cafe, his friend spotted a safe on the other side of the counter and said, "Did you ever open a safe?" Number 14 answered, "No." "Well, we can open this one."
>
> Apparently no. 14 had been somewhat reluctant, but that night they came back and "We hammered it open." They were caught at this and sentenced to the Prairie Penitentiary.

The neophyte's learning consists in part of an understanding of what one can reasonably expect police to do in specific situations. By providing opportunity for the observation of police behavior, the delinquent experience forms the basis for future reaction to the police:

> Anyway, I go up and they (the police) say, "Your partner's given us his version of your story, now tell us what you know." Well, I didn't go for this, because being brought up in the slums and that, I was suspicious of anything they said, without even knowing this tack that they used—this ploy that they use. I was just naturally, I wouldn't believe anything they said anyway. Because it was a conditioned thing in me from that environment. That they were bad and you didn't believe anything they said. (no. 11)

Delinquency is also associated with the reformatory experience, which seems to be a first formal step in the direction of the criminal career. Not only does it segregate the delinquent from his nondelinquent peers, but reformatory conversation, as my respondent's comments indicate, centers around crime, perhaps even more than in jails and penitentiaries. The following is quoted from my notes taken during an interview with no. 11:

> Number 11 goes into a long discussion on card tricks. He mentions that he worked in a factory for three years and did part-time stealing on the side. He started using drugs and was arrested for illegal possession of narcotics and sentenced to six months in a reformatory, and in there he felt his criminal education began: "And I went to a reformatory, and in there I would say my criminal education began, partially, that is."
>
> It is interesting that although no. 11 had been consistently engaged in delinquency and crime, and was recognized in the factory as one associated with the criminal element, he states that it was in the reformatory where he got "educated": "In the shop that I was working at, that is, in the reformatory, I got talking to one guy about laying notes. And he showed me a couple of ways of laying notes, and explained to me how lucrative it could be. And various other ways of B & E, heel man. . . ." (no. 11)

Number 27 states that, in 1943, he spent six years in a penitentiary, and that before this term he committed a wide variety of offences. In referring to the penitentiary sentence, he says:

> Well, incidentally, that's where my education in determining my future—I think you'll agree that up till now I was rather aimless, which I was, you know. But actually, I had grown pretty bitter in there—I done a lot of time in the hole. I must have done thirteen months in a stretch in the damper. And got my ass paddled—when I came out, I was determined to get hold of a bank roll. My first experience was with the military. This time—by this time, I was relatively broke—I had maybe a hundred dollars—and I had *no contacts* because I had been away too long. And I had to go to work. But before I could get—got to work, I had to get clearance from the army. And I got my call-up notice, and was rejected for medical psychiatric reason. (LAUGHS AT THIS.)
>
> I got cleared with the army and—and I worked in the shipyards as a rigger until I could get back on my feet. Now here's where the narcotics begins. (no. 27)

The above quotation indicates that, despite having committed a wide variety of offences, no. 27 considered himself as "aimless." By this he seems to mean he had not yet established any skill identity. This corresponds well with our previous definition of the "bum." The six year penitentiary stretch resulted in what we might call "career crystallization." He was bitter and determined to be less aimless regarding crime. This determination was hampered by the fact that, having been in prison for so long, he had lost his previous contacts with other offenders. Both for reasons of finance and association, he worked legitimately until "I could get back on my feet." At that point, he had developed connections with a drug trafficker who wished to use no. 27's skills as a burglar. From here on, his criminal activities, as well as his associations, took on a routine pattern. He was known by twelve of the persons I interviewed, and was clearly considered a "rounder."

C. THE PRISON AS SCHOOL

People who criticize prisons for failing to rehabilitate criminals frequently assert that despite a variety of approved training programs, prisons are essentially schools of crime. Such criticism finds support in testimonials to be found in popular magazines, among other sources.

In an anonymous letter to the editor of *Playboy,* a person awaiting trial states:

> . . . our jails are turning out more criminal minds than they are taking in. During my own confinement, I've already learned how to mix nitroglycerine and how to "peel" a safe, and I've been given some tips on the kind of weaponry to be used during an armed robbery— and I haven't even been sentenced yet.[3]

Disagreement as to the criminal schooling received has to do with the form, rather than the substance of instruction. As no. 30, an older inmate, implies, the school model, with a teacher-student relationship is inappropriate:

> That's a fallacy—this *teaching* of crime. There is nothing systematic —the majority of older guys with any self-respect or common sense— they don't go around telling anyone what they've done. If they're telling stories, they are stories in the first place. (no. 30)

Inmates think of such learning primarily in terms of "contacts" or associations that facilitate crime upon release. They agree that the techniques of crime are not ordinarily systematically taught in prison, but rather communicated informally. As such, the teach-

3. Letter to the Editor, *Playboy* 16, no. 8 (August 1969): 48.

ing and learning processes are closely related to patterns of association within prison. The example below indicates some of the ways
in which informal associations lead to discussion and fairly specific
advice as to how a crime should be committed:

> YOU WERE NOT AN EXPERIENCED CRIMINAL AT THAT TIME? No. HOW
> DID YOU KNOW WHAT WAS A GOOD BANK? Because of the time I spent in
> ———— (name of prison). I would look around, and we're sitting there,
> two guys that were in for bank robbery. They would say, well—he
> would be talking to his partner, for example, and I would be sitting
> there, and maybe I'd know him, you know—sort of and things like
> that, so he would call me over close to them, and he would say, "Well,
> Jesus Christ, you remember when we done that job, what mistake we
> done. We just should never have gone through that road, you know.
> We should have known better, or we should have known that there
> would be a road block there. We should have known it." And things
> like that. So, you know, well this guy should have known that, okay.
> Now maybe I learn by the misfortune of others, you know. Through
> these guys, now. And so, eventually, . . . One that I communicate
> with best, and I will be walking back and forth for hours with him,
> talking about possible ways of doing banks, you see. And how we
> could outsmart the people, how we could react to certain circum-
> stances during a bank holdup, and things like that. And if people try
> to get out of a bank, like a guy wants to come to you, and where to
> put your gun, and how to behave, you know. During a bank holdup
> to make it successful.
>
> SOME OF THESE THINGS YOU WOULD DISCUSS RIGHT IN PRISON? Oh yes,
> definitely. I SEE. SO, IN A SENSE, YOU HAD A LOT OF THEORY. Oh yes. Now,
> all the theory I required during the time I was in prison. On the out-
> side, I would think, and it was just a matter of refreshing my memory
> for one evening, for example, with one guy, and we're ready to put it
> into action, our theory. YEH. Or to a new bank, or whatever we had in
> mind. (no. 28)

Another example, from notes taken during an interview with no. 40,
also underlines the importance of friendship and association as a
prerequisite to learning crime in prison:

> Number 40 feels he learned the theory of safeopening beginning
> at the age of seventeen, during his first penitentiary sentence. He
> stated that he made a point of seeking out people whom he had heard
> about through conversation; he would then show an interest in be-
> coming friends with these persons. Much of this theory was com-
> municated in informal ways; for example, the newspaper would re-

port a safecracking job. Number 40 would refer the article to a safecracker during group conversation and say, "I wonder how he done that?" The safecracker might explain how the act was possible; number 40 would "milk" him for as much information as possible.

Number 40 noted that any specialized criminal is very reluctant to communicate this special knowledge; they are very suspicious: "It's the only thing he really has." It is this special knowledge that has made them a success and they don't want to part with it.

Before a safecracker will talk to someone he must be convinced of the person's "solidarity." I asked no. 40 what was meant by that term, and he stated the criteria in this order: he must not be an informer, he must be intelligent enough to be able to use this knowledge, and the safecracker must feel that perhaps he might be able to use this person to his own advantage later on—perhaps as a partner.

These criteria, said no. 40, mean you must become a friend of the safecracker before he will tell you anything. This friendship, however, is not sentimental, but is based on the solidarity referred to above: "The safecracker would probably watch you for a couple of months—they won't try to impress the mediocre type of individual." At the same time, the safecracker desires recognition from persons he respects. (no. 40)

Number 24, a safecracker, stated that at present the following skills were being "taught" at the Western Penitentiary: safecracking, check forging, B & E, robbing a bank, boosting, and, possibly, pimping; he felt that, in some sense, how to become a con man was also being taught, but of this he was not sure. He would personally never talk to a stranger about his own skills; he would have to know the fellow inmate for some time first, and such an inmate would have to be a "responsible type," which he defined as "at least twenty-five years old, probably thirty. Not someone reckless, not a young punk, you know—a stable character." Asked to elaborate, he said:

Well, I'd want to be sure that he'd be responsible about it, you know, not stash the nitro where kids could get at it, keep it out of reach—not be careless. Also, some guys put too much grease in, just to blow the whole thing to pieces. Well, that's no good, you got to take care not to put too much in, not too little. Some guys just make a big mess, that's not responsible.

WOULD YOU TEACH A RESPONSIBLE GUY ALL YOU KNEW? Yeh, probably, but he'd have to be the right guy. It used to be harder, you know, when I learned, it was tough to get anybody to say anything; they didn't want competition. I picked most of the stuff up on the sly—

just by keeping my ears open. Some guys are different too, you know—
like ———, he won't talk to nobody. Just keeps to himself. (no. 24)

Number 24 also said that he would not teach his skills to anyone
who was not mechanically minded:

I've tried the artistic type, but they can't do it good. Take ———,
that's his trouble—he's not mechanical, that's why he's not too good.
(no. 24)

Prison provides a setting in which the responsibility, loyalty, and
solidity of younger criminals can be tested without undue risk to
the older, experienced criminal.[4] Inmates are repeatedly subjected
to situations in which loyalties are at stake. The "solid guy" will not
"squeal," will take a "bum rap" rather than incriminate others, and
indicates, by his behavior and attitude, that his allegiance is to the
inmate culture rather than the administration. Reflecting the conflict of generations in the larger society, older criminals feel that the
younger generation of criminals are of inferior potential. Solid
types, it is complained, are hard to find.

Now, I wouldn't hurt you and I wouldn't hurt anybody. I don't
believe in this, you know. It's the same here around this institution—
most of the old-time thieves are fine, but some of these younger guys
will twist each other, because this is what they learned. I don't blame
them, but we were brought up in a—a school of crime where you
didn't rob another thief; you didn't hurt an individual and you had
certain codes that you lived by—you didn't finger anybody even if
you got a bum beef—you didn't inform on anybody—you rode it, you
know. Nowadays, it seems that the first guy to holler gets off and the
rest of the guys go to jail, but like I say—I do blame them in a way,
in the other way I don't because this is the way they were taught—
this is the way kids are brought up nowadays. (no. 29)

The following account shows how a younger inmate demonstrated his solidity to experienced criminals. Number 32 was sentenced to five years at Prairie Penitentiary. Being under twenty-one,
he was assigned to the young convicts section.

You know—nobody had got out of there till he's finished his sentence or until he turned twenty-one, but I made my mind up that I

---

4. The prison test, however, is not definitive. One must know a man in prison
as well as outside, to know what he is really like. An older respondent said,
"You meet a guy in prison, then you meet him outside, maybe you go on a caper,
then you know if he's alright." (no. 1)

was going to get out of there. There was what you call a segregation shop, a shoe shop, and we'd always watch them going by—the shoe shop was where all the tough convicts were—and they were all safe-crackers. And some of the best safecrackers in all of Canada were in that shoe shop.

. . . So I—it took me, let's see—it took me about thirteen months to get into that shoe shop. I was in that shoe shop when I was eighteen because I had made up my mind I was going to be in there.

YOU MOVED FROM THE YOUNGER CONVICTS? I did about eight months in the hole, and lost five months in remission in doing it, because the warden was just as determined as me, that I was going to stay in there. So I finally won anyway—I got into the shoe shop.

NOW, IN OTHER WORDS, YOU MADE ENOUGH TROUBLE FOR THEM SO THEY FINALLY GAVE YOU . . . Anything, that's right. I got into a little minor, you know—did a little hole time during these two and a half years, but nothing like previous. AND YOU WERE IN THE SHOE SHOP FOR TWO AND A HALF YEARS. Uh huh. And I learned safecracking from A to Z in here, in theory, in that shoe shop. There were approximately—oh, I'd say fifteen good safecrackers. Now, don't get the idea that they volunteered this information, you know. YEH—I WAS JUST GOING TO ASK ABOUT THAT. Oh no, no—they didn't. They all watched in effect, six months, to see just what type I was, and I had to—you know—how determined and how solid I was. And they finally got to like me and I learned from there on.

BY "SOLID," AND SO ON—WHAT DOES THAT MEAN? That means, you know—I wasn't running to the Instructor or anything like that, you know. I was a great con. Those days everything was black and white, too, you know. I mean there was no in between—you—those days you just talked to cons. You didn't talk to guards if you were an inmate. I SEE. Now, like today it's entirely different in this way. Any-time you talk to a guard, this only means he's telling you to do some-thing. Now this shoe shop, like I said, it had a gun cage right at the end, and it had an instructor and it had a disciplinary guard who did nothing but patrol. Round and round—on his entire eight-hour shift. Now, you weren't supposed to leave your bench.

SO HOW COULD YOU GET THIS INSTRUCTION WITH ALL THIS? During exercise period you could walk around—in those days exercise con-sisted of handball, horse-shoes and running. SO YOU ACTUALLY GOT YOUR INSTRUCTION DURING EXERCISE PERIOD. Right. Then there was two smoke periods too, you know—like when we had a—you could only smoke during a ten-minute interval in the morning and then ten minutes in the afternoon, and then you could leave your bench, you know. (no. 32)

This account also suggests that, when the inquirer is adequately motivated, learning can take place even in situations specifically designed to prevent it. It is obvious, moreover, that the learning of crime can occur in situations specifically designed to teach alternatives to crime. The quotation below implies that a legitimate training program suggested new criminal alternatives to the student.

WHERE DID YOU LEARN TO DISTINGUISH BETWEEN THE DIFFERENT TYPES OF ALARM SYSTEMS? Well, I just looked at them—I guess I heard different talk about alarms when I was in jail. TALK OF ALARMS IN JAIL? DID YOU IN ANY SYSTEMATIC WAY STUDY ABOUT ALARMS ANYWHERE? Well, when I was in the correctional institute, I took an electrical course for awhile. (LAUGHTER)

DID YOU TAKE THAT COURSE WITH THIS KIND OF THING IN MIND? No, no—but I got to thinking about it. And the books were there, and I started looking through them, to give me an idea of how they worked. (no. 2)

In-prison training in legitimate trades may be deliberately exploited for illegitimate purposes. As the following quotation indicates, many of the skills associated with building trades, widely taught in prisons, directly help the criminal improve his criminal activity.[5]

WHERE DID YOU LEARN THIS? Penitentiary. Everything I learn't was in the penitentiary! (LAUGHTER) You know—and other things, like, actually, I'm a qualified sheet-metal man—I never worked at it, but the instructor here will tell you, and the instructor at the pen will tell you, that I know more about the sheet-metal trade, more than they do—because I went into it deeply. I got the books—I learned how to use the acetylene torch and everything else.

DID YOU DO THIS CONSCIOUSLY, WANTING TO USE IT FOR ILLEGAL PURPOSES? Oh yes! Like I told you—everything I tried to do was to better myself in the field of crime.

SO YOU TOOK SHEET METAL WORK AND FOUND IT USEFUL. WHAT ABOUT OTHER TRADES TAUGHT HERE, LIKE CARPENTRY? Carpentry? You learn how a building is built and like ———— and I—our favorite entry is through the roof. . . . (no. 29)

5. Although the relationship of builder's skills to burglary is evident, the relation between prison programs that emphasize social skills and crime is subtler. Such programs may be particularly useful to criminals who use overt techniques. Inmates believe that the decision of the Penitentiary Service to terminate all Dale Carnegie courses in penitentiaries is a recognition of its potential for misuse.

Prison opens up new work possibilities, both legitimate and illegitimate. Recidivism rates suggest that the illegitimate alternatives are the more probable. It is clear that the prison experience expands the range of the criminally possible. A burglar, who changed from sneak thieving to live house-prowling was asked why he had not begun the latter, more lucrative practice, much earlier in his career:

> 'Cause I never thought of it then. It wasn't until I come in here that I heard different guys talking about it. So I thought, well . . . DID YOU LEARN ANY OF THE SKILLS HERE IN PRISON? Well no, there's no skill really; it's just from hearing over and over the guys talking about it. You know, prowling apartments and that, so I tried it on a house. (no. 21)

Prison provides the time and opportunity to enhance already existing criminal skills. A safecracker limited to nonexplosive techniques learned how to use explosives while in prison:

> HOW DID YOU KNOW HOW TO BLOW A CAN? Well, uh—this was incidentally the first time I had blown one—I—we used explosives, but —uh, from, you know, talking, my knowledge previous to going into the pen, of punching cans and cans in general, and talking to the various, you know, experts in the field, and then, in the pen itself, and that's where I learned how to make nitroglycerine, by the way. IN THE PEN? Yeh, in the pen. UH HUH.
> NOW, HAD YOU ACTUALLY PUNCHED QUITE A FEW CANS BEFORE THIS? Not quite a few—possibly half a dozen. FINE. NOW, IF YOU LEARNED HOW TO MAKE NITRO AT THE PEN . . . Well, theoretically, at least . . . HOW DID YOU MAKE OUT THE FIRST TIME YOU ACTUALLY TRIED IT? (LAUGHTER) . . . funny!
> (Number 27 STATED THAT HE HAD TROUBLE WITH HIS FIRST ATTEMPT TO MAKE GREASE BUT THAT THE SECOND ATTEMPT WAS A COMPLETE SUCCESS). (no. 27)

Number 36 insists the associations made and the expertise gained in prison are essential to the criminal career:

> HOW DID YOU FIRST LEARN TO OPEN A LOCKED DOOR? Well, I don't know, like, when I first started, it was just more or less—I don't know. I'd hear something mentioned, but once I got in jail, I learned to do things a little better. That's about all you hear in jail, how to do this, and watch for that, and how to get a car and change plates and everything. If you're going to become any kind of professional at all, you'd have to do some time—maybe some guy has run into some guy that's done

time and he hooked up with him, but otherwise it's impossible.
REALLY? YOU COULDN'T JUST LEARN ON YOUR OWN? Well, maybe you
could—I'd say you couldn't, myself. (no. 36)

Prison also provides a context within which various criminal alternatives can be explored theoretically, and some, such as con
games and violence, actually practiced. Through comparison,
thought, and the practice opportunities available to him, the inmate may choose a criminal trade most compatible with his own
abilities:

> In Leavenworth you got some of the highest-class criminals—I'll say,
> in the world; from the roughest type to the smoothest type. So you've
> watched them, you've found out how they've come ahead, and you
> start to use your own head a little bit. You find out what you're
> capable of and what you're not. You begin to see a little more clearly,
> you get a better perspective of things. You know you can do certain
> things and get away with it; other things are out of your sphere. You
> have time to see that.[6]

Respondents agreed that the adequacy of prison learning for
actual practice varies with the type of crime. A bank robber pointed
out that safecracking can be learned more fully in prison than
bank robbery because safecracking is more mechanical, whereas
bank robbery depends more on practice.[7] At the same time, he
added, only experience will tell a safecracker just how much grease
to use on any particular safe. In other words, the image of the prison
as a school of crime can be more accurately conceptualized by recognizing the variations within crime and how these demand different teaching contexts.

None of my respondents suggested any degree of specialization
before their first prison sentence—it was during prison that the
illegitimate career took on form and structure. Prison helps the
criminal realize that the haphazard and impulsive character of delinquency can no longer be afforded. As the teenager becomes an
adult, he needs to make greater efforts to avoid stiffer penalties.

Through association with experienced criminals, the offender is
introduced to, and has some basis to assess, alternative modes of
crime. He realizes that not all criminal modes are viable alterna-

---

6. Martin, *My Life in Crime*, p. 140.
7. Respondents provided several examples in which exprisoners' first jobs
(safe-jobs), based entirely on prison "theory," were completely successful.

tives. An assessment of his own abilities, qualified by his prison experience, provides direction quite different from earlier, impulsive peer-group pressures. He learns that some skills cannot be developed simply through the process of trial and error; he will need the help and confidence of those more experienced. Prison provides the opportunity for such association.

D. ASSOCIATION, LEARNING, AND EXPERIENCE

The association among criminals outside prison is not purely social. As in the legitimate order, in which associations between businessmen, laborers, and so on, are both social and work-related, so also considerable information relevant to criminal activity is passed along informally as criminals meet in places such as "rounder hotels."

The recipient of such information has much to lose if the information, whether received within or outside prison, is inaccurate; he might be exposing himself to unknown and unnecessary risks. In order profitably to use such information, he must be able to evaluate it correctly. The delinquent and prison experiences are useful, perhaps even essential, for this purpose.

To illustrate how such evaluations are made, it is helpful to look at work information that is more formally exchanged on an economic basis. Such arrangements may vary from a single tip-off to a more permanent arrangement between the criminal and his "finger-man." The financial arrangement, too, may vary from a percentage of the possible take, to a set fee for the advice.

Known rounders could "draw heat" if they do the casing themselves. Using a finger-man is, essentially, a division of labor and risk; also, a finger-man is important to nomadic criminals who haven't time to pick up information through local gossip. To rely on finger-men is no reflection on the casing abilities of the thief— it is simply acknowledging the fact that some persons, like bartenders, have access to more information than others. Furthermore, for purposes of his own safety, the criminal must be able to assess the merit of the finger-man's advice. Many novice criminals make their mistake by following poor tip-offs, and there is, apparently, no shortage of persons willing to give poor advice to younger "punks" for a percentage—if the caper is successful, the finger-man gains; if not, he has lost nothing.

As the following quotation illustrates, the inexperienced criminal is at a distinct advantage if he has wide criminal associations that enable him to assess advice in terms of the reliability of the source and the overall soundness of the proposal.

> Well, if it was a straight tip-off, if somebody said, "Well, I know a spot," and it wasn't having anything to do with himself, usually I'd be pretty leery, and unless I know the person,[8] I'd say, "Well, what— why should I waste my time by going out there looking at it." But if the guy comes and tells me, you know, "I know it's there, it's this— this type of safe, this type of alarm system, if any," you know—"the money is there on certain days," [9] well then I would go and see and if it was a thing where maybe it was a straight tip-off, maybe for ten per- cent or something, he wouldn't be coming along. But if somebody would come to me and say, "Look, I know a spot, but I can't get it, so do you want to come along with me?" Yeh—then I would take him.
> WERE YOU EVER TAKEN ADVANTAGE OF WHEN YOU WERE STILL INEX- PERIENCED? No, I—in one respect I kind of got an advantage—I had pretty well grown up with thieves and rounders. Well, because my old man's a rounder, see? . . . My old man had a liquor store on ———— Street for years and years—I lived right in the bootlegging joint. (no. 2)

In those cases in which the relationship between the finger-man and the criminal is impersonal (for example, they may be relative strangers), the criminal will take an added precaution:

> You always tell the guy you won't take it—so they don't know when. He may have told it to several. You wait until after doing it so he won't finger me. These guys go around looking for their end. (no. 15).

In other words, criminals expect that, if a stranger gives them a tip-off, he has probably given this same tip-off to others as well. The

8. The reputation of the source is one of the criteria. Later no. 2 adds that he would be suspicious ". . . unless it's somebody that I know knows what he's talking about. Has a reason to know what's there." That is, the information is evaluated in terms of how "reasonable" it is—the connection between the source and the information must be credible. In response to the question, "How do you distinguish between those who know and those who don't?" he said, "Well, a guy says to you, 'I know a spot—the building supply joint.' Well, now I *know* there's money in the building supply joint. . . . If it sounds feasible, I might examine it."

9. The specificity of the information is another criterion.

criminal will routinely "decline" the offer, thereby protecting himself from suspicion should the caper be pulled off by someone else
before he gets to it. However, should he decide to do the job, he
must communicate this to the person who tipped him off, immediately following the caper—it is assumed that his advisor would
eventually discover who did it, and that he must be paid.

The following is an example of a safecracker having a formal arrangement with a finger-man:

> Uh—but I was goin' to tell you something else too. We're getting a
> little ahead here. The—after this—oh, about 1940, late forties, we got
> in touch with a couple of finger-men. What they call finger-men. One,
> ———, was one of them, and he—I guess you know, was found on
> the golf course with his head blown off, in Vancouver a few years
> back. ——— was a beer-parlor waiter and he used to move from town
> to town. But his pastime was to—he made money fingerin' jobs for
> safeblowers. The phone would ring and it would be ——— from
> Penticton, or Vernon, or someplace where he was workin' in a beer
> parlor. When he had a score lined up, and for a quarter of what we
> used to make; the deal was that he would get one quarter of what was
> in the safe—he would phone us and tell us about this place and when
> the money was goin' to be there—he worked for two or three months
> in the beer parlor in the town and he'd line up two or three places
> in the town for us, and we'd go out and blow them and come back
> to Vancouver. (no. 29)

Enforcement of the economic arrangements between criminals is
not, of course, subject to civil law, but rather to informal norms and
unofficial "policing." It is clear that the criminal subculture can no
more rely on violence to enforce promises than the conventional
society can rely on the courts to enforce its contracts. Violence, like
the courts, is a last resort—the criminal subculture, like the larger
society, relies on relationships of trust and reliability. When conflict arises, as in the example below, the notion of "the reasonable
man" is invoked. In addition, external evidence by way of newspaper reports are introduced.

A burglar recalled how information he received from a finger-
man had been only partially correct. He had not paid the finger-
man the agreed upon two hundred dollars. I asked how the finger-man had reacted to this:

> Oh yeh—I left that out. I'm glad you asked that. While I was in
> jail charged with this thing, he was phoning my friend—my girl friend

and harassing people that I know, for this thing. Threatening to kill me and so on and so forth. And all kinds of threats about what he was going to do, 'cause he wasn't getting his money. 'Cause it was never mentioned in the paper how much money was there, and so he thought there was that amount. So when I got out, as it happened, he had got arrested for something else. So I know when I got out, he wasn't around.

WHAT WOULD HAVE BEEN THE EXPECTED PROCEDURE ON YOUR PART HERE? WOULD IT HAVE BEEN THAT AS SOON AS YOU GOT THE MONEY, TO GO TO HIM AND TELL HIM? Yeh—right. Yeh, that's what's generally done if things pan out. But the thing is, you see—I was hot, because all the information he had given me was rotten. You see, the money wasn't even where it was supposed to be, and so there's why I didn't contact him. You see, there was two doors to go through, so much of the information was incorrect. So I didn't feel that he had held up his end. So I didn't contact him or phone him or anything. (no. 11)

The above example is an illustration of several additional points: although in theory the arrangement was for a fixed price, it was in fact regarded as being proportionate to the anticipated take. Since the take was less, the payment was considered too high. Further, no. 11 was disappointed that the newspaper failed to corroborate his claims to a lower amount. He was aware that criminals use newspapers for various specific purposes. They may be used by the finger-man as an indication of the amount stolen, even though criminals agree the reported estimates of loss by theft are exaggerated:

Of all the smaller places I ever hit, they always put the amount up by a couple a hundred dollars, you know. They pay a pretty high insurance so when they get a chance they like to even things up a little bit. HOW WOULD YOU KNOW THIS? Well, these are ones I was caught on, and it comes out at the trial. (no. 36)

On the other hand, the criminal may rely on the newspaper to provide an assessment of what he has stolen—for instance, when the score must be planted hastily and left for some time before being counted, or when the theft consists of articles or securities whose value is unknown to the criminal.

The criminal will, however, need more help than he can get from newspapers; likewise, the trial and error method, although useful and common, imposes limitations. At some point, experienced advice will be needed:

ALL RIGHT—AND SAFES—WHAT ABOUT THOSE? Mostly from experience.

The square-door safes, they're all pretty easy to open, and—we heard talk about the one type of round-door safe and another there and it's just a matter, you know. Well, maybe we hear that so-and-so got a round door. Well, if you know the guy well enough, and maybe you've stolen with him, you go up to him and ask, "Well, how did you get that?" And if you know him well, and he thinks that you're going to make use of it, he'll tell you. WOULD THAT BE IN PRISON OR OUT? Both. BOTH—I SEE. (no. 2)

The account above indicates the ongoing nature of the learning process, before, during, and after the prison experience. Respondents suggested that on-the-job training or apprenticeship is unusual. More common is a gradual progression, beginning with awkward juvenile efforts, refined by the prison experience, and followed by trial and error combined with informal, intermittent advice from the more experienced.

None of my respondents who were known as safecrackers had been given on-the-job instruction by an experienced safecracker before having attempted some safecracking on their own. When early attempts at safecracking take the form of group efforts, such groups usually consist of equally inexperienced persons. The following respondent referred to such attempts as safe*breaking* rather than safe*cracking*: ". . . before, when we started going, we were pretty crude—four or five of us at a time." (no. 35)

Such efforts are characterized by the use of the simplest mechanical techniques possible. Because these simple techniques are applicable only to certain types of safes it is important that the would-be safecracker be able to identify these "easy cans." Such information is assimilated by association with more experienced criminals, both inside and outside. At the point when the criminal begins to refine trial and error methods by systematic study of specific techniques, one could say that a "career choice" has been made.

Members of a robbery gang also tend to be equally experienced. An armed robber states:

CAN YOU TELL ME HOW YOU GOT STARTED ON THIS—GROCERY AND DRUG STORES? Well, I met a man a little older than myself in a flophouse— that was run by the city. This was in the depression days and who instigated it I wouldn't have the faintest idea. I was the one that originally got a gun from a third man, and I had to pay a rather exorbitant amount for it at that time; and we started stealing cars, sticking up groceries, drugstores, and were eventually caught on a

jewelry store. YOU AND THIS OLDER MAN? Well, when I say older—he
was a matter of maybe four or five years older. NOW, HAD HE HAD
EXPERIENCE IN THIS KIND OF THING? No—he had none. SO YOU BOTH
STARTED OUT, AS IT WERE, GREEN. Yeh. (no. 27)

Such statements belie the popular-media picture of the smart
leader followed by a group of stupid thugs. The experienced criminal, wishing to maximize safety and security, prefers to work with
the most reliable and experienced persons available. The inexperienced, therefore, must gain their experience with others equally inexperienced.

Nevertheless, although the practice is unusual, the experienced
rounder may systematically train someone to whom he has taken
a liking and in whom he has confidence.

NOW AFTER YOU GOT TO GET GOOD AT THIS, HOW DID YOU SELECT GUYS
TO GET TO HELP YOU, OR WHOM WOULD YOU TRAIN AND WHOM WOULD
YOU NOT TRAIN? Well, you don't really train anybody, or you just go
with your partner, you see—or you go with any other one of your
friends that wants you to go with him. Or if you got a score, maybe
your partner don't like it so you go with another guy—like I said,
safecrackers then—well, you kind of understand each other—*you knew
that each one knew as much as you did.* . . . But as far as goin' and
trainin' somebody—no. But some younger fellow might come along
who doesn't know anything about it and you might take a likin' to him
and he might take a likin' to you, and he might hang around you,
and bug you into seein' how it's—how you do it, and so you, finally,
you might take him along with you, and tell him what you know, and
show him—and you wouldn't select anyone—I mean the person would
have to come up and ask you and have to be a good friend of yours.
(no. 14)

Again:

HOW DID YOU GET ———— TO TEACH YOU HOW TO BOOST? Well, he took
a liking to me. I really don't know—it's just that one day he was stuck
without a partner; he asked me to come along and I came along and
he thought I had done alright, so from then on it was, as a matter of
fact, his partner went to jail, and I just continued on with him. (no.
20)

The most common pattern in learning crime is illustrated in the
following account from notes taken during an interview with a
safecracker.

Prior to doing his first "can," no. 4 bugged an older safecracker in prison ". . . until he finally divulged how to do it." This instruction, he added, was ". . . not like a teacher-student, it was just a matter of discussion during work."

When he left the prison, he went back to his regular partner and described to him what he had learned about safes. His partner said this was ridiculous, but no. 4 persuaded him to come along: "I followed the instructions to the letter. It opened—we were both overcome with it all—the ease of it all!

This first job had been a punch job—technically the simplest. Following this no. 4 and his partner ". . . opened many doors by trial and error." He would study the door after opening, if possible: "The list of safes we knew how to open grew." This went on for four years; they had not as yet used explosives, nor had they ever been caught punching safes. They became increasingly eager to try explosives since they found so many safes that couldn't be opened in any other way.

During this time, no. 4 was associating with other safecrackers; he stated that he was known as a safecracker and was putting on that he knew all about it. He eventually asked another safecracker whether he could borrow some grease. "I wouldn't admit that I knew nothing about it." He obtained the grease and chose a small safe, but was unsuccessful. The next day, he discussed his problem with some more experienced safecrackers. He found he had used too long a fuse and was advised to use electric knockers. This he did with success. (no. 41)

In this chapter, I have argued that the learning of technical skills takes place, basically, by experiment and experience. Formal teacher-student relationships are rare; partners in crime, whether experienced or inexperienced, tend to be equals. I have indicated that prisons are schools of crime, particularly in providing associations with other criminals who may later choose to work as partners, or who serve as advisors both during and following the prison experience.

Technical skills are useful to the criminal only if he understands the contexts in which they can be used. Someone able to use a cutting torch might be able to open a safe in his garage, but he is not therefore qualified to open safes for purposes of theft. Similarly, the reader of this study, who has been given considerable detail as to, for example, safecracking, is not therefore equipped to become a safecracker. The prerequisites for success in crime include many social and perceptual skills, difficult to describe and not likely to be learned from a reading of their analysis.

6

"CASING"

Perceptual Skills

A. INTRODUCTION

It is not enough to be skilled in technical matters only. The successful safecracker must be more than a mechanic, the armed robber more than a gun-man. In addition to the required technical skills discussed in the previous chapter, the criminal must possess a variety of perceptual skills pertinent to his trade.

Some of these skills are common to all members of society—by mastering and refining them, making them relevant to his work, the criminal simply extends the legitimate order to serve his illegitimate ends. He shares with legitimate tradesmen a particular sensitivity toward those aspects of the everyday world that affect, or are affected by, his work.

The criminal's perceptual skills are theoretically interesting. A social structure depends in part on communication, on consensus as to the meaning of symbols and often subtle cues. These symbols, necessary for the routine functioning of a society, are ordinarily designed for well-meaning persons who will interpret them as intended; however, they also provide information to those wishing to use them for purposes *not* intended.

Knowing this, the legitimate order is constrained to devise cues to mislead the malevolent, yet not confuse the benevolent. The criminal must be able to recognize opportunities within a context deliberately constructed to conceal such opportunities. To do so he must be able to distinguish between those symbols intended to mislead him and those intended for others. Depending on the type of crime intended, this requires varying degrees of sophistication in interpreting the square, routine, everyday world. The crime itself is perpetrated, as it were, on square soil, in the legitimate world. The criminal must take on the role of the "other" in order to take advantage of the civilian. Although it is apparent that such role-taking is necessary for the successful confidence game, its importance in other types of crime is not recognized in related academic literature. Sherri Cavan has noted that:

> The taken-for-granted character of the standing behavior patterns of any setting may also become a matter of practical interest to those who wish to exploit them, to use them in a way that is neither routine, nor proper, but nonetheless possible.[1]

I am suggesting that, insofar as the typically "unquestioned background of things taken-for-granted" is a matter of practical interest to the criminal, his observations may bring the taken-for-granted to the attention of the civilian.

B. REINTERPRETING THE CONVENTIONAL

The concept of casing,[2] usually thought of as preparation for a specific caper, may be broadened to include the more general observations the criminal makes that bear upon his work. The criminal's mentality consists in part of a complicated rating system that includes countries, states, provinces, cities, suburbs, down to specific companies and businesses. England is believed to be an easy place for safecrackers because it is thought that the English still use old-fashioned keyhole-type safes. Since they are largely serviced by the same safe companies, the United States and Canada vary in terms of alarm systems rather than style of safe. It is thought that of all

1. Sherri Cavan, *Liquor License* (Chicago: Aldine Publishing Co., 1966), p. 6.
2. "Professionals agree that casing is far and away the most important part of laying out a heist (robbery). . . . As used in the underworld, the word means 'gathering information from observation.'" DeBaum, "The Heist: The Theory and Practice of Armed Robbery," *Harpers,* 200 (February 1950): 70.

west coast cities, Vancouver is the most highly bugged. Certain towns are not good for any type of crime because of few roads or mountainous terrain: "you can't get out."

Towns and cities may also be rated according to size, the evaluation varying according to the type of crime being considered. Small cities of fifty to one hundred thousand population are considered good temporary spots for shoplifting, but not for permanent shoplifting: "Small towns good for a run pass-through—people ask if you work there." (no. 3) That is, in small towns people inquire about one's work habits.

Burglars appreciate the absence of security systems in smaller towns; and bank robbers, the absence of strong police contingents.

After spending some time in Vancouver, "looking around," a burglar decided to stay in Vancouver. He had "looked the place over from Tswassen to North Vancouver" and noticed that a large number of business places were bugged. He also observed that "there was not much in safes—so many safecrackers had gone over them so often. The good ones [safes] that are left are in the Interior and in the North Western United States." (no. 35) He said he knew several men who operate out of Vancouver, but who do all their jobs outside the city. He also noted there were very few American safecrackers. I asked why and he said, "I don't really know—it seems they would rather pick up a gun." (no. 35)

The preceding discussion indicates that the criminal, like the tourist, the farmer, or the potential new resident, makes evaluations on the basis of factors relevant to his interests. Many of these factors are of more general concern: for example, noise, traffic flow, and the lack of privacy in small towns, and are of interest to the potential new resident as well as to the criminal. Sensitivity to these constitutes part of the general socialization process to which both civilian and criminal are subject. It is the more specific socialization, such as occurs in prison, that sensitizes the criminal to the relevance of these factors to criminal activity.

Information the thief finds relevant to his "work" may be parts of conventional conversation rituals; for example, the housewife meeting the deliveryman at the door is expected to offer an explanation for not having the payment in her hands, even though it would be odd for her to come prepared in this way. If, when apologizing for the delay she indicates that she had to go all the way up to the bedroom for the money, she has provided important information to be used later by the deliveryman, or passed on by him to others.[3]

Number 15 notes that a fairly common method of getting information is to become friendly with the cleaning personnel, who are unaware they are aiding a criminal.

> Buy them a beer. . . . They're on the verge of starvation anyway. . . . Give them a line by saying that you have a small business of your own and might consider having it cleaned. Before long they'll ask you to see what kind of work they're doing and they take you along and you look around. (no. 15)

The criminal may also find he can safely and efficiently use legitimate means for disposing of stolen property. What could be more innocent than a laundromat bulletin board?

> (I THEN ASK NO. 35 HOW HE WAS ABLE TO GET RID OF THE GOODS HE STOLE, AND HE REPLIES:) Well, let's put it this way. I had no trouble getting rid of it. There's different ways. Let me give you an example now. If you've got things that people like, for instance now, a good portable typewriter, the best place to sell that would be to just walk into a laundromat and you type up a little thing, saying "portable typewriter for sale," and you put down your telephone number. There are people in there washing their clothes and they—well, they give you a phone. Now these people look up at that board and they see all the stuff that's there. Half of that is stolen goods. (I QUESTION THIS AND HE SAYS:) Oh sure, it is, sure. That's just an opinion now, but I would say, when I think of how I used it—like I—I put ads in the paper too, things like that. (no. 35)

Even the weather may have special meaning to the criminal. It may facilitate crime directly, as in the muffling of noise, or indirectly: various social conventions related to climatic conditions, are seen by the criminal as being conducive to certain types of crime. An armed robber (no. 41) noted, for example, that one can run down a back alley at any time without being conspicuous, but that one cannot run down a main street or sidewalk except on a rainy day. For this reason he preferred to do his robberies on a rainy day. Another armed robber noted that for bank robbery: "A stormy day is good, 'cause there's not too many people on the street . . . and you can wear a raincoat and—to carry a shotgun." (no. 36)

The routine features of various occupations such as armored-

3. Martin, *My Life in Crime,* p. 67.

truck driver, merchant, salesman, are of central importance to the criminal. The ordinary citizen has only tangential interest in, for example, how the businessman handles his money. When the citizen discusses this as part of conversational small talk, the criminal pays special attention:

> Like on this ———— (place that sells cars)—I got tipped off on this and so on and it was by a girl that worked there—she didn't even know it when she was telling me. She just happened—she didn't actually know. She just happened to mention in conversation that this company had been down and bought so many trucks and they paid cash for them. And this is all I had to hear. (no. 29) [4]

Even when legitimately employed, the criminal will be alert to crime potential:

> (I ASK A QUESTION AT THIS POINT ABOUT HOW HE GOT TO KNOW THE FELLOW, AND HE SAID:) Well, I met him at the pen. He was from Ottawa—that was his home. He got out ahead of me. Now, *in the course of one of the jobs he had held* as a delivery boy—he had worked for this company, on Saturdays and weekends, doing deliveries —he knew that the drugs were out there, and the price of them out here. And he knew that this could be converted into a lot of money. (no. 27)

Sensitivity to various symbols of one's occupation has been noted in people with legitimate occupations, such as janitors and workers in auto industries. Such sensitivity, which takes on the form of habit, is common to illegitimate occupations as well. A safecracker had just listed some of the essentials of casing: looking over the place, seeing where the safe was, what type of safe it was, whether it had been repaired, what the volume of business was, and so forth. He then added:

> I still have the habit—automatically my eyes go around the room, see if there is a safe there. I see it and note what kind it is—I have to drag my eyes off it. (no. 4)

Respondents agreed that perception increases with experience, yet the degree of consciousness employed while casing diminishes. The experienced safecracker seems to come upon his "victims" by

---

4. The naïveté of the square girl is in contrast to the sophistication of those who are "wise." When I asked no. 22 how he explains the source of his generosity to his girlfriends, he said, "they know enough not to ask questions, the kind of girls you go out with on these trips." (no. 22)

accident; he seldom can account for the factors that led to his discovery. He does not deliberately look for a score—he just "spots"
them. Although experienced criminals may be relatively unconscious of the casing processes in which they are engaged, the dimensions of what seems to be intuitive can be documented.

During one interview no. 2 mentioned that he had been tipped
off to a good potential score in a city one hundred miles away, and
had driven out to look it over. Although he argued that his techniques for avoiding the police were simply "natural," they imply
learning and experience:

> BY CAR? Yes. With my car—a U-drive, or somebody else's. We'd go
> up there and . . . NOW WOULD YOU BE FOLLOWED, ON A TRIP LIKE THAT?
> Well, I'd pretty well make sure that I wasn't followed. AND HOW DO
> YOU DO THAT? HOW DO YOU MAKE SURE? I'd drive around. You can tell
> when you're being followed. YOU CAN? Oh yes. You should be able to,
> anyway. OKAY, TELL ME HOW YOU KNOW THAT YOU'RE BEING FOLLOWED?
> Well, you go up the freeway, you stop somewhere, see what happens.
> Sit in a beer-parlor for awhile. Watch the approaches, drive around.
> Then, well, you know—it's just a natural thing. You don't even think
> about it—you just know in your own mind—you make sure, you know
> that nobody knows what you're doing—you know. (no. 2)

The personal investigation done by criminals may consist of
casual looking, specific search, or both:

> CAN YOU DESCRIBE SORT OF A TYPICALLY SMALL GROCERY HOLD-UP FOR
> ME? Well, just in the normal course of living in the city—we would
> spend our days walking around or on the street-car or so forth, and
> keeping our eyes open for various—for various locations that looked
> as though they would be the least protected, and have the easiest access
> to and to get away from, and there wasn't really too much deliberate
> planning, in the sense that occurred prior to—that is, as a matter of
> fact, sometimes it would simply be impulsive—we would just steal a
> car and then go looking for one. (no. 27)

A good deal of casing "happens" while the safecracker is going
about legitimate interests. One is more likely to encounter relevant
information in some places than in others:

> DURING THOSE TWO OR THREE YEARS—LET'S SAY YOU WERE GOING OUT
> ONCE EVERY TWO WEEKS. HOW MUCH OF THAT TIME WAS SPENT IN CAS-
> ING? Uh—usually we would, like I say, when we knew that we were
> getting low on money, we would start looking around. Now we may

have been tipped off—we may have been told innocently and we may have run into it. I've run into scores where I'd walk in and I'd be in there on a perfectly legitimate reason, and I'd see what was going on and you're—the average person doesn't look for—he might see a big bag of money and think nothing of it or not know what it is. (no. 29)

Although the experienced safecracker is always "looking," various factors, particularly his financial position, may necessitate some deliberate casing. For example, he cannot always afford to wait till something "shows up" or "comes along." Nor is it always possible to assess a potential caper leisurely. When the safecracker needs money quickly, he may deliberately need to find a spot, dispense with careful planning, and proceed quickly and at high risk. For this reason as well as others,[5] crimes committed shortly after release from prison, when the exconvict is out of money, are the most risky:

> This is what we found was the hardest part—stepping out of jail with no money and you have to go for this first one you find. You can't sit back and study it and find out how you get in. So you've got to make a first night's stand on it, where otherwise we'd sit back and— through the years we got so that, oh—we'd spend anywhere to a week sometimes, figurin' out a place, finding out what the alarms are, and the easiest method of getting in. (no. 29)

The criminal's more obvious perceptual skills have to do with those cues that tell him something about the location and availability of money. For example, no degree of technical sophistication will suffice if the technician repeatedly opens safes that are virtually empty.

The criminal is also informed of possibilities through continual association with other criminals. He is aware that the availability of money is not randomly distributed over any given period of time. Seasonal fluctuations in business, patterns of armored-truck pickups, police beats—all of these affect the availability of money and are largely predictable. In addition there is, as it were, a steady source of money—that is, there are numerous business establishments that can be counted on to have money throughout the year. The ability to predict the amount of money in a safe or cashier's till requires some knowledge of how business is routinely conducted.

Given a knowledge of these variations, the criminal can assess the

5. Other reasons include the fact that the exprisoner is probably on parole and known to the police as one just released and in need of money.

probability of a good caper at any specific time. This probability is generally not as high as he would prefer; consequently, he keeps looking for breaks, unusual opportunities, or a change for the better in the daily routine. The jewelery store he has long wanted to "do" is now being remodelled—how, he asks, does this affect his chances? If in his favor, the temporary nature of the opportunity dictates that he does not delay. Respondents noted that the criminal, like the legitimate entrepreneur, must learn to restrain his greed. A good opportunity ought not necessarily be taken advantage of—if he does not need the money at the time he may be better off not doing it. The more experienced implied that over-zealousness had been the downfall of many amateurs.

C. THE MISUSE OF SOCIAL CONVENTIONS

The safecracker cannot assume worthwhile economic potential in every safe at all times, but he may assess this potential by indirect factors such as the amount of cash business done plus the distance from the business to a bank. He will also check on the availability of night depositories. In addition, he may make a detailed study of the situation, frequently playing the role of the legitimate citizen:

> And during my fishing trips up there I'll run across certain things that I'm lookin' for, like this store here. I usually find that they don't bank their money—usually I'll find out from somebody that been through the town, some other heeler or somebody like this and they'll tell me—just in a matter of conversation. They'll say, "my Gawd, I saw a nice store." And you sit down and drink a beer or somethin', and he'll tell you about the ———— store (women's dress shop), a legitimate store (LAUGHS). So I went up there to the dress shop—I went fishing, and when I come back I decided to look at it.
>
> HOW DID YOU LOOK AT IT? I'd go inside, see? I'd have my girl with me or something. And I'd usually hand them a hundred dollar bill for something I buy. They usually don't carry this kind of money in the till—they don't like to, anyway. And they have to go to the office. Now that's all I need to know. If I see them go in the office I know the money must be there and the safe is there. I'd say, I'd say it's a way of doin' things, the way they work. Like, when I go, I'll carry three or four hundred-dollar bills in my pocket, just for this reason. Just to find out—if they can cash it in the till, fine and dandy—then I've got to find out some other way.

OH, I SEE. THEY ARE GOING BACK FOR CHANGE. Yeh. They're going
back to get change. They go into an office so that's where the money
is. Now, if I get serious about the place, I'll park across the street at
closing time and I'll watch them . . . I'll see where they go. If they
go home, fine. Next night, I'll sit there and watch them. Till I find
out when they deposit. Like, we sat out there and waited at the ———
(dress shop) to find out when they do deposit their money. It was a
Monday morning. So we went in Sunday night and blew the safe!
You know, it's more or less unconscious—just like a businessman. Like
a salesman looking for customers and he gets tipped—this store is
opening and so on and so forth, and like I say, it's a separate way of
life altogether from legitimate people—it is illegal, but it gets to be
a way of life so that you unconsciously—even when I'm not. . . . (no.
29)

The above example displays the thief's knowledge of several conventions. He is aware that men do not ordinarily enter women's
dress shops without a female partner and so he does not go in by
himself, since this might create suspicion (if not at the moment, then
certainly in retrospect). Furthermore, the thief treats as important
what the legitimate customer ignores or considers a nuisance. Going
back for change is common procedure—most customers try to avoid
such delay by trying to accommodate the cashier's need; the thief
deliberately invokes what others try to avoid, and interprets the
action not simply as "going for change" but also as "telling me
where the safe is." One respondent who had done many small-store
holdups early in his career would give a cashier a one- or two-dollar
bill for a pack of cigarettes, thereby obliging her to open the cash
register for change:

I know a lot of guys who couldn't get the cash register open. This
way I just put the gun on her right then. (no. 36)

The following example displays how the burglar correctly perceives that it is considered appropriate for a female customer to use
the washroom in a drugstore, but not for a male. Violation of this
informal, unwritten code of etiquette would arouse suspicion. The
popular notion of criminals as ignorant of social conventions is
negated by such examples of criminal sensitivity to very subtle social expectations:

NOW, HOW DO YOU KNOW IN A DRUGSTORE, FOR EXAMPLE, WHERE THE
SAFE IS? Well, generally speakin', it's in the back or if it's a round-
door safe it might be near a front window; they might have it in

sight, you know, so the police can watch it, when they drive by. I SEE. I would find it anyway. YOU WOULD FIND IT? Oh yeh.

HOW CAN YOU DO THAT WITHOUT MAKING YOURSELF CONSPICUOUS? Well, there's always people poking around joints, you know. If it was in—perhaps in the back, where ordinarily I couldn't go, I would maybe put on my old lady and say—probably want to use their washroom or something. They could give me a reader[6] what it looked like. And I'd pretty well be able to tell from what it looked like what it was. I SEE, UH HUH. Something like that would very seldom happen, you know—usually you can spot them. (no. 2)

Casing may involve activity that actually includes "setting up" a place to be "hit." The example below shows how the desired goods are picked out and placed in such a way that their pickup during the burglary is most efficient. The procedure may also provide the burglar with considerable pleasure:

Like we needed tires one time, so we went in and bought a generator in this junk yard. He overcharged us, but we didn't say anything. But we picked out four tires and we come back that night and beat him for them. When I go into a place, say like a junk dealer or something like this, now I say to my boys, "Know what you need," you know. "Go look for it and put it aside and put it aside and remember where you put it, while I keep the guy busy." I'll be talking to him and we'll be dealing, and my partners are getting everything set. So I know he's trying to beat me, and I'm laughing at him inside, 'cause I'm really beating him! (no. 10)

In order to steal from coin-operated vending machines, the thief may need to be highly sensitive to the habits of those who use the machines:

NOW IN THESE RESTAURANTS THAT HAVE THESE LITTLE JUKE-BOX PANELS ON THE SIDE OF THE TABLE, HOW MUCH IS IN ONE OF THOSE? Oh, on a good take you get maybe thirty-five, forty dollars. It all depends how much it's played. You see, it all depends on where the kids—so you can usually tell. Like when you go in a place you see a bunch of kids in there. They may have four booths in the back and in the front for the older people, so you know mainly where to go—the one's that the kids have been playing, and that's where you find you get your main take, if you can't get nothing else. (no. 10)

This thief assumes that one observation of the seating preferences

___

6. The expression "taking a reader" is used by criminals to indicate they are deliberately casing.

of kids in a restaurant is sufficient for the prediction of a pattern. When such observation is impossible, he assumes that preference for seating away from the front windows varies inversely with age. The seating preferences of cafe patrons by age, a matter of no conscious concern to the normal customer, is relevant to the thief.

As a further check on his assessment, the vending-machine thief pays attention to the sound of a coin dropped into the slot; this is more relevant to his interests than the sound of the subsequent music:

> Yeh—you see, if it falls, the bag stands about this high and about this wide, and then when it falls, if it falls a long distance, it's got a—well, a type of a sound like pinging sound, but when it's full, or almost full, it drops—it's got like a flat sound. You know, and you can tell. It takes a while to learn, but you can tell. And then you know if you want to hit this place. (no. 10)

While relating a particular caper, a safecracker indicated how he had played several roles during his casing procedures. In order to get a look at the safe, he pretended, with briefcase in hand, to be looking for a place to have some letters photocopied. Unfortunately for him, he was not granted admittance to the desired room. He then made a forcible entry at night:

> As soon as I looked, as I seen the can, I knew I'd never be able to get it with grease or other tools or any way. It was a class E can—that means it's a pretty fair can. (no. 25)

Next day, hesitatingly "admitting" that he was a bookie and needed a very good safe, he asked a safe salesman to show him their best. Again, unfortunately, their best did not include the type he was intending to "make." "But anyway, I seen enough down there to know very well that I would never get the money—it would take too many blasts." (He and his partner were eventually successful by buying off an employee who faked a robbery in order to protect his job.)

In some ways similar to those of the student of occupations, the thief takes an interest in the work roles of persons whom he would victimize. This may be for purposes of avoiding the victim, for managing and predicting his behavior when confronted, or for predicting how he will secure his valuables. An addict-thief (no. 2) made the following observation about the habits of druggists (quoting my interview notes):

(1) Since it is required by law, druggists will lock up their supply of drugs in a cupboard for the night. However, "Nine out of ten druggists leave the key in the lock." Why? Because drugs are cheap to them and easy to replace. Secondly, they know that if a thief wants drugs and enters the store at night, he will get the drugs anyway and will do a lot of property damage to get them, if necessary.

(2) Drugstores near medical buildings will carry a larger supply of drugs than will other drug stores.

(3) Druggists seldom keep their drugs in a safe. The reason—they know that if an addict cannot find drugs in the cupboard, he will open or take the safe. The latter may involve the loss of money and papers; the druggists would rather part with drugs.

(4) With the exception of cigarettes, drugstores have little merchandise that can easily be turned into cash.

(5) The addict-thief must know a bit about pharmaceutical terms in order to rob a drugstore. "Any kind of morphine will be taken— Demerol and Methadone keeps you from getting sick when you're wired [addicted]." (no. 12)

The addict-thief's comments show that he depends on *his* knowledge of the *druggist's* knowledge of the typical ways of the thief. In terms of game theory, the situation becomes, in Schelling's terms:

> . . . a behavior situation in which each player's best choice of action depends on the action he expects the other to take, which he knows depends, in turn, on the other's expectations of his own. This interdependence of expectations is precisely what distinguishes a game of strategy from a game of chance or a game of skill.[7]

The appreciation of legitimate work roles that enables the criminal to use them advantageously in the pursuit of money also enables him to "pass" as a "legitimate" for purposes of avoiding detection:

> I'd just leave town for a little while. I'd go down to Reno, San Francisco, Chicago, and blow it there for three weeks or a month. Then I'd come back here again and put on the old gumboots and green shirt, pack a little bit of beer and root it off around the beer parlors and pool halls. You see, draw steam off all the time. I used to go over to the beer parlor and I'd say, "What's the chance of holding off payment till pay day?" So I'd run up a bill here and there, at the pool hall, maybe three, four dollars. Well, the first place the police are gonna go is the beer parlor, the pool hall, and they'll ask, "Is

7. Thomas C. Schelling, *The Strategy of Conflict* (Cambridge: Harvard University Press, 1963), p. 86.

this guy hanging around here at all?" "Yeh." "Well, has he any money?" "No, no, he's got a case of beer here he hasn't paid off in two weeks." "Well, that can't be the guy we're after, then." (no. 7)

Relying on routine and established patterns and work-styles permits the criminal to operate in terms of what Sacks has defined as "the incongruity principle." He notes that police

. . . learn to treat their beat as a territory of normal appearances. The learned normal appearances are to constitute background expectancies in terms of which the beat is observed during particular patrols. Given these expectancies the patrolman must so sensitize himself as to be arousable by whatsoever slight variations appear which seem to be warrantable bases for making of the explanation of presented appearances a matter of investigation.[8]

Not only is it expected that the whereabouts of a manager is predictable, but the work-style of bank employees is constrained by certain predictable patterns of propriety. Number 41 stated that he once entered a bank to rob it, and noticed a man standing behind the bank counter with his foot on a chair and his arms folded. He knew this man was a policeman, so he left the bank without robbing it. Number 41 went on to explain that a bank manager may sit on a table with his feet hanging down, or sit on a chair and have his feet on a desk, but "he will never stand with one foot on a chair!"

The armed robber relies heavily on the routine of business arrangements as the basis for the predictions he must make. Like legitimate customers, he expects to see certain persons doing certain things in expected places and at expected times. However, unlike the legitimate customer who may make appointments to ensure the probability of seeing whom he will at the time he wishes, the criminal may need to rely on routine only, and this may lead to errors with serious consequences:

DO YOU CHECK AT ALL WHERE THE MANAGER MIGHT BE AT THE TIME OF THE HOLDUP? Aha, positively. That's why I was kind of shook up this last time. We went several times and he was always in his office, at that time, and the very morning we drew up he was standing by the counter, and he was the one that pressed the silent alarm. (no. 7)

The incongruity principle also permits the criminal to pass as a

8. Harvey Sacks, "Notes on Police Assessment of Moral Character," in D. Sudnow, ed., *Studies In Social Interaction,* New York: The Free Press, 1972, pp. 284–85.

"normal" even while in the act of committing the crime. He is aware that persons within bureaucratic structures know that "lay people" are generally confused with any specific system and its rules—the criminal capitalizes on the tolerance for error adopted by those "in the know":

> And I started out on the heel, and the live prowl. Now these are two different things. The heel, well—the best way to explain it to you is that I used to go out at nine o'clock in the morning. I always dressed in a suit, to look like a businessman, and I used to always carry a briefcase, which, you know, looks very respectable. You know, it's a key to practically any place. So, what would I do—I would hit certain office buildings around the noon hour, and, you know, I generally had sort of like a paper route mapped out in my mind. You know, these office buildings—I would hit big office buildings. So I would walk down these hallways in these big office buildings, and at noon hour quite often the receptionist, she'll go out for lunch and she'll leave the petty cash box there. And I would just proceed along these hallways in these buildings and go into an office and if there was nobody there I would go behind the counter and if possible go over the counter, and if there was cash there, I would take it, and go on to the next office. And if someone walked in at the time, well generally I would look at the roster of names, you know—in these big business buildings they have these signs with names, "Mr. so-and-so," and generally I would try to remember at least one name for each floor. And if someone did come in, I would say, "Well, pardon me, could you tell me where Mr. so-and-so is?" and I done this, and this was fairly lucrative, because I was just handling cash. I don't like merchandise. And I was also working the live prowl. (no. 11)

The following account by a thief who specialized in doing the live prowl [9] in hotels, shows how he takes advantage of the license associated with a businessman's convention. To do so he literally plays the role of the businessman at a convention. The account is taken from interview notes:

> The hotel prowler should book in during a convention week and get himself a convention badge—they can usually be had for very little money, or the burglar can make his own. When he goes to bed, he should set his alarm instead of having the desk waken him. He

9. The live prowl is burglary that forms an interstitial category between those crimes in which the victim is avoided and those in which he is confronted. That is, the live prowl necessitates latent skills that must be immediately available should victim confrontation occur.

should go to work at about four in the morning, and, preferably, work with a woman partner. Both should be well-dressed, the man wearing the convention badge and the woman carrying a large purse—"with only enough in it to make it look legitimate should there be trouble."

Just before leaving his room he takes a couple of shots of whiskey: "so you have whiskey on your breath." This is done in case the occupant wakens—the burglar then pretends that he is drunk and has entered the wrong room. He will even insist, if necessary, that the door was unlocked. Number 12 added that he would be normally treated as a convention brother and cheerfully helped on his way.

The burglar and his companion then proceed to "run the hotel down." This means that the burglar begins on the rooms at the top floor and works his way down. This is a safety precaution—if anyone's suspicion is aroused, his pursuers will be above him; not below, where they might prevent his escape. (no. 12)

The surreptitious criminal gives scant attention to the interaction between himself and the victim, except in terms of how to avoid such interaction. Here again, he relies heavily on the predictability of the victim. It is assumed an employee's presence at his place of work is based on business routine rather than spontaneity. Number 35 pointed out that if one was intending to burglarize a business at night, one should check the business precisely a week before the time of the intended caper, "to see if anyone works late on that day." Not only is it assumed that such business demands requiring someone to work late will be repeated, but that they will be repeated on a weekly schedule.

D. THE ASSESSMENT OF RISK

In addition to having assessed the probable economic gain to be had on a potential caper, the criminal who is casing must weigh the relative degree of risk as well as the technical difficulties involved. Usually, the assessment of economic value precedes the assessment of risk. A safecracker may, while on legitimate business, spot a particularly "easy" safe. He may then assess the probable economic value of the safe's contents. Whether the value is high or low, if the risks are low, he may "make" the safe. On the other hand, if both are high, he may also attempt the job. We are assuming, of course, that other factors, such as his need for money, are similar in both cases.

Generally, the perception of risk varies with whether one works surreptitiously, as in burglary, or openly, as in robbery. The thief perceives of risk as being the relative probability of avoiding the victim and the police. The robber, on the other hand, intends to confront his victim—his risks center around the probability of successfully managing his victim while avoiding the police.

The degree of risk involved varies with the type of crime, but, in addition, different crimes are more dangerous at different stages. The safecracker's greatest point of danger is the actual safeblowing. Once this is done, he leaves with the cash—a relatively "safe" loot. The burglar out for merchandise faces high danger when making his exit and again when disposing of the goods; the house burglar must be careful during the entry, and the bank robber faces his greatest danger at the point of departure from the bank.

1. The Victim's Perspective

The assessment of risk in victim-confrontation-type crimes tends to focus on characteristics of the victim and on the prediction of police behavior. In order to predict the victim's behavior, the criminal must look at the crime from the victim's point of view. For this reason, criminals associate the risk factor with the relative importance of the money to the victim, rather than with the absolute amount of money under consideration. For example, the reasons for avoiding the corner grocer are complex,[10] including considerations having to do both with the amount and its importance to the grocer:

> YOU WOULDN'T LEAVE OUT THE CORNER GROCER BECAUSE YOU FELT SORRY FOR HIM? Well, no. That might be in the background—part of it; but the primary thing is that it's not worthwhile. These corner grocers, they get hit a lot by armed robbery, but it's not a question of armed robbery. These are kids: they're not drug addicts or anything like that. . . . a lot of corner stores are dangerous—I would not want to try to run-in one of them. (no. 32)

As no. 32 suggests there are economic reasons for avoiding the corner grocery—the generally low-profit yield is not worth the risk. Holdup

---

10. One reason may be the question of status involved—the safecracker, for example, cannot use his skills as a safecracker at the corner grocer's. He knows, from personal juvenile experience, that corner grocery stores are "done" by "kids."

of the corner grocer is seen as being extremely dangerous as well—
the grocer cannot afford to lose even one day's take and so he may be
desperate and dangerous:

> In a store, if you take two hundred dollars, you take away a man's
> life savings—he's going to fight—he is dangerous. Not in a bank. It's
> not because it's his life savings—that didn't bother me at that time.
> (no. 41)

The robber differentiates between victims in terms of how likely
they are to resist theft. Such a distinction is made partly in terms of
whether the property belongs to the victim, or has been entrusted
to him by others. Although he expects greater resistance from the
property owner, he is also prepared for resistance by the property
manager, despite feeling that the latter's resistance is irrational.
Criminals cannot understand why anyone would fight for money
that is not his own and that is insured. Further, given their own
readiness to use violence, they conceive of resistance on the part of
the victim as nothing less than "stupid." "The only people that'll
give you any trouble is some ignorant guy fightin' for his boss's
dough.[11] Bank robbers expect to be most successful when dealing
with highly experienced bank managers and depend heavily on the
rationality of the manager to make their robbery successful. In bank
robberies, they perceive of rationality in terms of the victim's complete compliance. The victim is dangerous to the degree he sub-
scribes to current conceptions of bravery, even though it is not his
money being taken. Bank robbers are afraid of younger male employees—potential "World War Two heroes," and prefer older bank
managers: ". . . with grey hair—the younger ones may give you a
fight." (no. 39)

The quotation below illustrates the points made above—the quiet
confidence of the bank manager is apparently reassuring to both
customer and robber:

> The manager plays the key role. WHAT DO YOU LOOK FOR IN A
> MANAGER? Well, usually if he's a middle-aged, he's usually pretty calm.
> They don't have a tendency to rush you. They'd be well versed, that
> is—if they're held up, just do as you're told and nobody will get
> hurt. Sometimes you get these young managers in their late twenties or
> early thirties. And he figures, "Well, maybe I'm a judo expert and
> maybe I can catch this guy." You never know. But the older they

11. Martin, *My Life in Crime*, p. 37.

are, they seem to be more stable, more reliable. They're not too anxious to finish up on the flat, you know what I mean. They're quite reliable, you see. They're middle-aged and they figure they've got a family, and, after all, all the money is insured, so why should he step out, you know what I mean. That's what we have a law for.

I'M OFTEN AMAZED AT SOME OF THE THINGS THESE MANAGERS DO. Very foolish, very foolish. I was extremely fortunate in that no one has ever followed me, but if they had done so, I would never—I would have shot. I would never stop—I would have shot. (no. 8)

2. The Police

A knowledge of police routine is important for some types of crime and not for others. The hotel prowler does not need to pay any attention to police routine and the house burglar needs pay only scant attention. In such crimes in which it *is* important, the actual casing of police routine appears to range from methodical preinvestigation, to simply watching for police during the caper and avoiding being seen by them. Accounts of casing procedures varied. One safecracker recalled how he and his partner would sit on a tall building near a Safeway store they intended to "make." After several days of watching the police routine from the building, they were ready to proceed. More common, however, is a less systematic method, which respondents found difficult to articulate in any more detail than to say, "You watch for the police, see whenever they make their rounds." This watching for the police consists of a complex series of visual clues not readily observed by the layman. As such, the clues resemble those by which policemen distinguish a suspect from a regular citizen. The experienced criminal can spot an unmarked as well as a marked police car.

Burglars who enter business establishments must be alert to police routine. They must not be seen making the entry, or be noticed on the premises. Unless the "in" is difficult and time-consuming, burglars do not consider evading the police as problematic at this point. They may simply park on a nearby street until they see the patrol car or patrolman pass by. If the entry is made by picking the lock, the burglar will need to know whether (and how) to close it after he is inside. For this reason, he needs to know what the particular habits of patrolmen are—do they simply drive by, do they walk by and try the door, or do they use flashlights to look in the windows? Such details form a part of the general knowledge of burglars who remain within one city, and need not be ascertained for each particular caper. When in strange territory, however (particularly in small towns), the burglar will want to acquaint himself with these details beforehand.

> No, I'd probably—if there was a spot to hang around I'd probably hang around and see how they—the harness bulls around there would check the place out. Whether they knock doors or whether they get out of their car or . . . OH, I SEE. HOW DO YOU DO THAT? Well, try and park—well, in sight of it. Maybe in a hotel parking lot, or—some spot that's a little inconspicuous, much as you can. You get an idea if they got a regular routine. (no. 2)

A nomadic burglar must make certain general assumptions regarding police routine. He does not have the time or the contacts to carefully assess police behavior in the various towns he passes through. The following quotation illustrates such general assumptions:

> Oh, I'm not afraid of much going wrong in something like this because very rarely anything will go wrong. You may run into a cop maybe, by chance; like, you may be coming around and there's always a chance of someone passing by, but like I say, I try to do the places along the highway and on the edge of town, when possible. It's very rarely I go in the town, because that way I bypass all these hazards. Because when the cop goes out to the edge of town, he don't stay out there; he goes back in. And you very rarely find people walking around the edge of town. (no. 39)

The safecracker, in particular, needs to be cognizant of police routine. He cannot afford to set off an explosive just as the patrolman goes by. The chief function of the safecracker's partner, the "point-man," is to indicate when the coast is clear for an explosion. The use of a point-man, however, also depends on location:

> (Number 15 POINTS OUT THAT USING A POINT-MAN CAN BE HAZARDOUS:) It's not only the police you've got to worry about but the population as well. There might be a neighbor and he sees the point-man standing in an awkward position. I'd say you have to worry more about the population than the police if you've got it cased right. (no. 15)

Casing for police routine is also paramount in the bank robber's preparation. Since he fully expects to be followed or stopped by the police, he must be able to predict the time of pursuit and the loca-

tion of roadblocks so he can either avoid the police or be prepared
for the confrontation:

> So we drove to that place, and the bank was nicely situated, whereby
> we had four roads where we could get away—four roads, and the
> police would likely come to two roads, because by their patrolling,
> you know—they patrol certain areas. And I've watched their way of
> patrolling that area, a certain area, and I knew that at a certain hour
> they would be in that area, and the two immediately available roads
> connecting to that bank would be situated in the way, I felt—you
> know. So I decided that our getaway would be in the direction of
> opposite them, and which we done—and we went through success-
> fully. (no. 28)

A good bank must have a good "out," implying that the robbers
will be able to leave the bank and go in a number of different direc-
tions. Although it is unlikely they will alter their prearranged getaway route, the alternative routes are intended to mislead or dis-
perse the police. I was told some bank robbers inform one another
as to when and where they plan to work. By synchronizing their efforts, each group gains the advantage of police dispersal.

If the bank is located in an urban area, it should also be located
next to a moderately busy street. Congestion of traffic would delay
the robbers and sparse traffic would make the getaway car too conspicuous.

E. CASING: PLANS AND PRACTICE

Despite the general agreement among criminals as to the necessity and fundamentals of casing, it should not be assumed that these
requirements are routinely met. Various factors prevent adequate
casing. A criminal may be well informed about, and experienced in,
adequate casing and preparatory measures, yet still find it incon-
venient, or impossible to implement them. In order to survive, he
is forced to compromise, yet in doing so he runs his greatest risks.
Shortage of money and time are major reasons for compromise:

> Where I made the mistake, though, is I was never out long enough
> so I could plan a good one (bank robbery), like where I could get a
> couple a hundred thousand, and then just stop, but you don't just
> step out of prison and get that kind of money—you need six months
> or a year's planning. (no. 36)

Since the "in" is of central importance to the burglar, and often technically the most difficult aspect of his work, the availability of an easy "in" may dictate his work routine. Occasionally, the favorable aspects of an "in" are temporary and subject to change. They may demand quick action, thus bypassing careful planning:

AND WHAT ABOUT—DID YOU EVER PICK A PLACE SORT OF ON IMPULSE? Oh yeh. WITHOUT ANY PRELIMINARY INVESTIGATION? YOU JUST SPOT AN "IN" AND GO IN? Yeh—but it's a rarity at that. I mean, there'd be some basis for it. Maybe at some prior conversation in a group; like I said, safecrackers are—they discuss things with each other and they might say, or I might say, "I saw something." Like that one time in ——— a guy was telling me about a score while sitting in a beer parlor. He was working as a mechanic at that time. He'd spotted this, and we done it that night. He had information they were doing some remodelling at the back. They had these scaffolds, right up. He said it'd be ideal, which it was. (no. 32)

In the above example, the "in" was temporary—removal of the scaffolds would have made the job impossible. A routine feature of construction, for example, the erection of scaffolds, is seen by the criminal as an opportunity for crime.

The criminal is seldom, if ever, in a situation in which he can commit the "perfect" crime. Like other humans, he works in a state of compromise between the ideal and the real. Here also, as in conventional society, some, for reasons of differential abilities and opportunities, must compromise more than others. Still others may compromise for greed or recklessness. In either case, the cost is high.

7

CONCLUSION

In each of the preceding chapters, the immediate implications of the data and analysis were spelled out with reference to the general objectives set forth in the opening chapter. In this concluding commentary, I shall elaborate on some of the wider implications of this study.

The reader familiar with related literature can now assess the extent to which this portrayal confirms, or calls into question, previously held assumptions and models of criminal behavior. The reader may also compare his own conceptions with the picture presented here.

The data presented here are not intended as a comprehensive description of crime. In fact, although the attention to detail may imply otherwise, it cannot be considered a complete and definitive picture even of specific kinds of crime, such as safecracking or bank robbery. The reader who wishes to use the data as a primer on crime will find it deficient; it is intended for the analyst rather than the practitioner.

The data are further limited, though at the same time strengthened, by the perspectives that developed in the early stages of the research—most important, the desire to test the utility of applying an occupational perspective to criminal behavior. In addition, the reader is reminded that subjects were selected from those known as experienced property offenders; whether the findings can be applied, for example, to occasional offenders, remains problematic.

The analytical issues that the descriptive details illustrate, however, are not restrictive. Instead, they facilitate comparisons between various types of crime and between criminal and noncriminal behavior; for example, by careful attention to the behavioral dimensions of crime I have shown how such concepts as specialization, professionalism, apprenticeship, and work satisfaction may help us understand criminal behavior. Such concepts, taken from conventional work roles, can seldom be applied without modification; nevertheless, even where the implied behaviors and processes are largely absent, for example, in systems of apprenticeship, the concept itself sensitizes us to the more general issues—in this case, the various learning relationships that do exist. It was shown that an increasingly complex technology encourages criminals to specialize; nevertheless, despite a sample of respondents, most of whom had settled into preferred types of crime, the shifting from one type of crime to another indicated a degree of flexibility not normally evident in conventional, specialized work roles.

The work perspective draws attention to the various skills and abilities required of persons in various conventional work roles. The presence or absence of specialized skills is commonly used to explain wage differentials and work satisfaction. I have argued that a recognition of the various skills required in criminal activity may, likewise, help explain variations in status and work satisfaction among criminals. By carefully looking at safecracking skills and their meaning to practitioners, it is obvious that a purely economic model is inadequate—some of the rewards of crime have to do with the satisfaction inherent in craftsmanship, for example. The model of a criminal as one who takes a craftsman's pride in his work, and who applies his skills in the most profitable way he thinks possible, is very different from that model of the criminal as one who gets his kicks out of beating the system and doing evil. This is not to say that persons fitting the latter model do not exist; nor should description and explanation be confused with justification. The morality of crime, whether committed routinely and dispassionately, or in spiteful glee, is another issue. It is important, however, that we hold our conventional morality in temporary abeyance, so we can begin to understand the meaning of criminal behavior to those who practice it.

Throughout this study I have emphasized both behavior and the meaning of this behavior to the actor. The importance of the sub-

jective perspective resides in the ways it helps to explain the behavior of those who define the world in that particular fashion.
The reasons why miners go back to work following a mine disaster
are more intelligible when we listen to how they view their alternatives. Such an approach may also help us understand why a person
may return to crime following lengthy prison sentences. We may
still reserve our right to make moral judgments, but we will not
be as likely to invoke notions of the bizarre and pathological.

The actor's perspective also alerts us to the significance of taken-
for-granted aspects of everyday life. Common problems take on new
meaning; the absence of a parking spot in front of the bank is an
inconvenience to the shopper, but it is of central occupational concern to the urban bank robber. Variations in everyday arrangements
take on special significance—a painter's scaffold left up overnight
becomes a means of entry to the building for the burglar. We are
reminded that, although the meaning of routine behavior may appear most obvious and unequivocal to us, it may have quite a different
meaning for others. For example, the ordinary customer is merely
annoyed at having to wait when a cashier must go back to the
office for change; to the burglar this is an indication that larger
amounts of money are kept in the office. The sociology of occupations has alerted us to the ways in which different occupations and
work roles give rise to worker perspectives that are specifically work-
related. The assumption that it is the illegitimacy of crime rather
than its specific work demands that gives rise to a criminal perspective, has prevented a similar occupational approach to the study of
crime.

The criminal's ability to reinterpret commonsense knowledge in
ways relevant to his work suggests both continuity and discontinuity between the socialization patterns of criminals and noncriminals.
The ability to make profitable, albeit illegal, use of everyday knowledge suggests a continuity in the socialization of criminals and
noncriminals that is not developed in the literature on crime. Success in crime, no less than success in legitimate enterprise, requires
that the practitioner be a good student of social patterns and arrangements. The systematic application of this knowledge was illustrated in our discussion on casing procedures.

The criminal's work requires that he be sensitive and informed
as to what is going on in the world around him—his work does not
permit him to use his subculture as a form of retreat. He cannot

work in secluded places; he must go with the traffic, for that is where the money is. His work is done in homes, banks, and places of business. Whether his act of crime is committed surreptitiously or openly, he must be familiar with his work context, the habits of its people, its usual and unusual processes. The criminal cannot be ignorant of social convention lest he draw attention to himself and to his intentions. In addition, he must understand the nature of conventional work roles and routines in order to exploit them. Further, such exploitation may demand that the criminal use work habits strikingly similar to those of the ordinary worker. As was indicated, criminals themselves recognize the similarity between the rounder and the square-john with reference to such work-related matters as punctuality, reliability, and doing one's work with care and diligence. Conversely, the criminal bum, were he to apply his style to legitimate work, would be no less a bum.

Attention to the details of criminal behavior has enabled me to expand the sparse literature dealing with the learning of crime. Although it is recognized that the criminal's skills are learned, few researchers have attempted to document *what* it is that he learns, and *how* such learning takes place. As indicated above, much of the criminal's learning is not unique to criminals. He, like other men, must be able to communicate in the prevailing language, understand the rudiments of business transactions, probably be able to drive a car, and so on. It is in his ability to relate such conventional knowledge to criminal behavior that his learning becomes unique. Even this statement must be qualified in recognition of the fact that the civilian, too, by knowing the rules of the game, is somewhat equipped to break and exploit them. It is probably more accurate to say that it is the refining and focussing of this knowledge that makes the criminal's learning different.

I have shown how this learning is facilitated during periods of delinquent behavior, an age when everyday conventions are not yet fully taken for granted; their potential for misuse and manipulation is, therefore, more obvious. Indeed, it seems unlikely that an adult conventional citizen could fully enter "rounder" status without early delinquent experiences.

In addition to an elaboration of these perceptual skills, I have discussed the implications of the more technical, manual, and organizational skills required for the execution of various crimes. Crime is more than attitude; the requisite skills can be described and their learning traced. I have shown that the method of learning criminal skills does not resemble the system of apprenticeship common in legitimate skilled trades; criminals usually work with equals, whether experienced or inexperienced. Some mechanical skills are learned by formal instruction from the more experienced, and I have indicated how and why some skills are more easily learned in prison than others. Indeed, some of the skills useful to the criminal, such as those of the building trades, are learned from legitimate prison instructors, but applied in illegitimate ways.

Although initially I did not intend to include an analysis of the prison experience, it quickly became obvious that the criminal's learning and work cannot be understood without reference to this experience. An analysis of learning processes and criminal association leaves the distinct impression that prisons are a part of, rather than in conflict with, the crime phenomenon. We are in need of studies specifically designed to assess the ways in which agencies and organizations ostensibly intended to prevent crime may have quite different latent effects.

An occupational perspective includes an examination of the ways work roles affect, and are affected by, social and technological change. The way the criminal initiates and responds to such change is of interest both for the study of crime and the study of society. From this point of view, crime is seen as an interaction between conflicting interest groups, rather than the isolated activity of subcultural enclaves.

This interaction sometimes takes on a simple stimulus-response pattern. The criminal's innovation and success generate opposition. When criminals learned how to blow ordinary safes, the manufacturer developed pressure bars. Such a pattern should not obscure resulting economic implications. The vast and rapidly growing security industry has a vested interest in the criminal's ingenuity. As criminals learn to open newer and better safes, the businessman's insurance costs rise, and he, in turn, is ready to purchase even newer and better safes. A conflict model that overlooks the ways criminal success is in the immediate interest of various economic and occupational groups would be misleading.

Many of the changes to which the criminal must adapt are part of social change in general, rather than a direct response to crime. Architectural changes generated by competition in the market have tended to be favorable to the criminal. The self-serve system has made merchandise easily accessible to both the customer and the shoplifter. The friendly, personal image now being projected by banks and loan companies has coincided with the replacement of austere teller's cages with low counters and open design. Bank robbers also find this arrangement more inviting.

Not all of these changes have been in the criminal's favor. The development and widespread use of alarm systems and the credit-card economy have made burglary more difficult and less profitable. The unintended and less obvious consequences of such changes need to be taken into consideration; I noted, for example, that by making burglary more difficult, we increasingly compel the criminal to obtain his money by robbery—a procedure much more dangerous to both the criminal and the public. It is obvious that increasing technical sophistication will not eliminate property offences, but that such change affects the form, if not the extent, of crime. It should be possible for a society to apply its technology in such a way as to discourage the most objectionable types of crime, rather than to make them the only profitable options for criminals.

Much contemporary research, particularly that having to do with the construction of typologies based on characteristics of criminals, proceeds on the assumption that knowledge of the criminal's background and characteristics will facilitate the control of criminal behavior. This approach need not be disparaged in order to make a case for alternative approaches. An occupational perspective seems to have obvious potential applied utility. To view crime as work demands that we look at it in terms of its viability as an occupation: skills required, training opportunities, effects of technological change, financial returns, and costs and risks involved. It may well be that the public would be more successful in the control of crime if it knowledgeably manipulated the work dimensions of crime rather than the practitioner. I have shown how architectural and technological changes may favor or impede various forms of crime. An occupational approach sensitizes us to these issues, and, in addition, helps us to see crime within the wider context of work and success opportunities in our social structure.

Theories used to explain criminal behavior range from broad general theories of human behavior to specific hypotheses applicable to certain types of crime only. This variation in theoretical perspectives may be partially explained in terms of the specific behavior under study. Julian Roebuck states:

> Any general theory of criminal behavior, given the current definitions of crime that include such different kinds of activity as drug addiction, murder, embezzlement, rape and treason, can hardly escape the necessity of being a general theory of human behavior.[1]

Roebuck suggests the criminologist turn away from the attempt to develop general theories and ". . . turn to the development and testing of a number of special theories."[2] The first step in this strategy, he argues, is the development of a "workable typology."[3]

Criminologists have had difficulty moving from the development of typologies to special theories. Typologies based on legal distinctions and designed to differentiate between criminals and between various criminal careers draw attention to the many possible variations, but generally fail to draw these together into manageable analytic units. What I have suggested in this study is that the analytic distinctions be made in terms of the behavioral dimensions of crime rather than in terms of its practitioners. In so doing, I simply follow the approach of the sociologists who study work in general.

Analysis of various forms of crime led to the distinction between surreptitious and overt crimes, categories that subsume numerous legal distinctions. Surreptitious crimes are characterized by the need for mechanical skills and a concern with victim avoidance. Overt crimes require organizational skills and concern with victim management.

By basing our analysis squarely on the behavioral dimensions of crime, with careful regard to the meaning of this behavior to the practitioner, the study of criminal behavior can be brought under the more general rubric of the sociology of work. In this way, the sociology of crime can become a less isolated scientific pursuit, drawing on and contributing to the theoretical development of the social sciences.

1. Roebuck, "The Negro Armed Robber as a Criminal Type: The Construction and Application of a Typology," in Clinard and Quinney, *Criminal Behavior Systems*, p. 375.
2. Ibid.
3. Ibid.

APPENDIX

Methodological Notes*

A. INTRODUCTION

Obviously, no study is possible unless the desired data are available. When the subject matter, however, involves secret information, then the factors that make such information available to social scientists are themselves sociologically interesting. What, for example, were the conditions prompting Williamson to speak with such freedom into Keiser's tape recorder? [1] We are given glimpses into Maurer's ongoing interaction with members of whiz mobs,[2] and of Shaw's counselling relationship with Stephen, the jack-roller.[3]

Given the nonshareable nature of such information, it is not strange that the careful and descriptive accounts of crime we do have are often the result of fortuitous circumstances, rather than deliberate plan. David Maurer's linguistic interests provided us, as a by-product, with the best descriptive material on pickpockets available. Relationships of trust and confidence were developed well before a number of researchers (for example, Sutherland, Shaw, and Keiser) initiated their actual research. In this appendix I indi-

* For a more complete account of both methodology and subject matter, see P. Letkemann, *"Modus Operandi: Crime as Work"* (Ph.D. diss., University of British Columbia, 1971).

1. Williamson, *Hustler!*
2. Maurer, *Whiz Mob.*
3. Shaw, *The Jack-Roller.*

165

cate how a series of circumstances enabled me to respond to the
need for descriptive research.

By way of an earlier study of the implementation of habitual-
criminal legislation in Canada,[4] I was granted access to two federal
prisons and was invited to attend the weekly Thursday-evening
sessions of paroled habitual criminals. Because of personal interests,
my attendance at these informal sessions carried on well beyond
the time of the initial study. Gradually, over a six-month period,
relationships with some parolees and parole officers developed into
friendships and mutual trust. I realized I was being confided in,
consulted, and treated in a way parolees do not normally treat
squares. I also realized I was being given access to information
otherwise unavailable.

My research was beginning, as it were, well before its formal inception. Many hours were spent in casual conversation while driving, eating, or other leisure-time activities. The evenings spent
listening to a group of "cons" exchanging anecdotes in their own
peculiar type of humor were particularly delightful.

The importance of this initial "socialization" period is underscored by those methodologists who emphasize the social aspect of
the interview situation. Later in this chapter I shall elaborate on
Cicourel's concern with the establishment of "systems of shared
meanings." He states:

> The well-conceived interview, complex as it may be, must have its
> roots in the categories of common-sense thinking, for without a
> knowledge of such roots the interviewer could not establish the
> necessary community for conducting his research. This means a
> recognition and understanding of how the respondent-interviewer
> interaction involves overlapping social worlds. According to Shutz,
> relevances necessary for the synchronization of meaning are pre-sup-
> posed. The respondent's and interviewer's stock of knowledge at hand
> and their definition of the situation will determine their mutual
> reaction to the questions posed.[5]

It is difficult, in retrospect, to place these associations within the
framework of what is commonly known as a research design, since

4. This study was requested and sponsored by the Canadian Committee on
Corrections.
5. Aaron V. Cicourel, *Method and Measurement in Sociology* (New York: Free
Press of Glencoe, 1964), p. 79.

at this point no research was intended.[6] My growing academic interest in the association had to do with the relationship of what I was hearing to the content of standard criminological literature. When I discussed my research interests with several parolee friends they assured me of their cooperation and indicated they would recommend others who would be helpful to me. A total of forty-five men were interviewed; some only once, others by repeated association. Twenty of the interviews were taped. In addition, I was able to draw on the resources of persons involved in corrections and custody, as well as persons who had a very direct interest in crime: namely, bank managers, store clerks, and the manufacturers of safes.

In order to assist the reader in his assessment of the data and interpretations presented, a brief, yet detailed description of the research procedure and situation follows. As Becker points out, the methods used in qualitative research are seldom made explicit.

> Qualitative analysis of field data are not new in social science; indeed, many classics of social research have been based on such analyses. But the methods of arriving at conclusions have not been systematized and such research has often been charged with being based on insight and intuition and thus not communicable or capable of replication.[7]

B. SELECTION OF SUBJECTS

As was indicated earlier, the initial subjects were those parolees attending the group meetings. It became obvious that some were better able to converse, or were more inclined toward communication than others. Whatever selection occurred here was not with research purposes in mind, but in terms of compatibility and friend-

6. There is a sense in which this period corresponds with what Becker, et al. have referred to as the "unstructured techniques" used by them at the initial stages of research. Such techniques are referred to as methods which would ". . . allow us to discover phenomena whose existence we are unaware of at the beginning of the research; our methods had to allow for the discovery of the variables themselves as well as relationships between variables . . . techniques in which the data-gathering techniques are not designed, for instance, to see which of two or more alternative answers to a question someone will pick, but rather which questions he himself will ask." H. S. Becker, Blanche Greer, Everett Hughes, and Anselm L. Strauss, *Boys In White* (Chicago: University of Chicago Press, 1961), p. 18.

7. Ibid., p. 30.

ship. Two persons in particular became close friends and contributed in the role of the "well-informed informants," [8] not only in terms of their own technical knowledge, but in terms of their ability to refer me to persons able to contribute to particular questions and interests I had. As my research interest developed, they introduced me to several persons they thought I should see, and these contacts, in turn, led to others.

Referral to persons outside of prison was done with caution—my informants would not embarrass or put in jeopardy someone, like themselves, whose concern was with the management of discrediting information. Most referrals were to persons in prison at the time. The practice of passing on greetings from the parolee to the inmate generally initiated a successful interview and usually led to inmate-inmate referrals as well.

The problem of gaining entry privileges to the federal prisons[9] was frustrating and time-consuming. The delays, however, do educate the researcher in the formal and informal power structure at the institution. Not only may the researcher be viewed with suspicion, which explains some of the hesitation on the part of prison administration, but he is also viewed as a nuisance, an interruption, and as someone who does not appreciate the routines and patterns that are part of the prison-as-organization. Once granted entry, I was given unexpected latitude in several important aspects, not the least of which was the freedom to select my subjects. This freedom was restricted only insofar as I might not see those persons in solitary confinement at the time.

In addition to specific referrals, I solicited help from personnel employed in various "correctional" capacities. In describing the type of person I wanted to meet, I listed only two criteria: first, he should have considerable experience in property offences, and secondly, he should be known to have a specific skill as a criminal (for example, safecracker, or bank robber). Such information is not readily available in official records, but is more reliably inferred from

8. K. W. Back, "The Well-Informed Informant," in R. H. Adams and J. J. Preiss, eds., *Human Organization Research* (Homewood, Ill.: Dorsey, 1960).

9. It should be noted that these institutions are part of the Canadian Penitentiary Service; as such, they are under federal rather than provincial jurisdiction. My use of federal prisons implies an initial selection—namely, persons whose sentences are of two or more year's duration. This choice was deliberate, in that my population was more likely to consist of recidivists and persons with serious offences, rather than with what are known as "petty offenders."

the inmate's prison reputation, in which distinctions of this kind, based on informal and unofficial information, are widely acknowledged.

It was difficult to know in advance how the research interests outlined in Chapter One could best be accommodated. Owing to circumstance, the first five persons specifically interviewed for this research were known as safecrackers. The cooperation of these subjects, and their willingness to provide extensive referrals, made the prospect of limiting my subjects to safecrackers only, highly attractive. However, on the basis of initial interviews it became apparent that by limiting my subjects to a single type, the analytic utility of my research would be seriously undermined. It became obvious that the category "safecracker," for example, cannot be understood without reference to numerous other categories to which the safecracker also belongs ("rounder," "B & E man," "thief").[10] Furthermore, testing the utility of applying conventional occupational concepts to crime would certainly be completer if more than one type of crime were studied. Indeed, the study of one type alone would be incomplete, since practitioners constantly make comparisons between various types of crime. Safecrackers, for example, see their trade as being quite different from that of "going heavy" (armed robbery). In addition, the study of more than one type facilitated comparison —a useful research strategy in any case, and particularly helpful for description and analysis.

As the interviews proceeded, the criteria for selection of further subjects became increasingly explicit.[11] Various skill categories became apparent and further selection of subjects was done, in part, on the basis of these skills. In this way, information could be supplemented where necessary. Further, as the interviews proceeded, the categories meaningful to the actors became apparent.

The persons interviewed are not necessarily representative of the larger prison population, or of criminals in general. In fact, my selection of subjects suggests my sample is biased in favor of the more skilled, experienced, and successful criminal, although, at the same time, it does not include criminals who have managed to evade the law.

10. The terms are defined in Chapter Three.
11. Wiseman discusses similar problems in her study of alcoholics. "In an exploratory study of this type it is difficult to know in advance what the sample should be representative of." J. P. Wiseman, *Stations of the Lost* (Englewood Cliffs, N.J.: Prentice-Hall, 1970), p. 282.

In terms of informal reputation (that is, the illegitimate activity by which the subject is "known" both to peers and persons in law enforcement), the forty-five subjects may be grouped roughly as follows:

Safecrackers	10
Armed robbers	5
Bank robbers	5
Breaking and entering	10
House and hotel burglars	3
Shoplifters	2
Theft: various forms	10
Total	45

The criteria as to the adequacy of the data are complex. Neither a complete picture of one type of crime, nor a representative portrait of crime, the research demonstrates the relationship between the "how" of some types of crime (given various technical constraints), and the context of expectancies within which such acts are committed. This requires careful and detailed attention to the behavioral dimensions of crime and the meaning of the behavior for the actor. Given these requirements, how is the adequacy of the data assessed?

As a rough guide during the period of data-gathering, Glaser's "saturation technique" was used:

> The criterion for judging when to stop sampling the different groups pertinent to a category is the category's theoretical saturation. Saturation means that no additional data are being found whereby the sociologist can develop properties of the category. As he sees similar instances over and over again, the researcher becomes empirically confident that a category is saturated.[12]

This technique was particularly applicable to the study of safecracking. The technology of safe construction limits the number of methods by which a safe can be opened. Although the procedures were discussed in detail with ten known safecrackers, by the time I interviewed the last three I was receiving no significantly new information.

The application of the "saturation technique" was more difficult

---

12. Barney G. Glaser and Anselm L. Strauss, *The Discovery of Grounded Theory* (Chicago: Aldine Publishing Co., 1967), p. 61.

in the case of armed robbery. Subjects indicated that numerous procedural variations are used. The data, as presented, are intended to illustrate the range of these variations. Although each subject was able to provide additional information as to procedural variations, subjects agreed as to the basic problem of robbery: managing the victim. It is this problem that makes the concept of "going heavy" or "armed robbery" meaningful to the criminal, and that distinguishes robbery from some other forms of crime. The data, therefore, must adequately represent victim management as central to armed robbery.

The criteria for the adequacy of qualitative data are not available in as explicit a form as are those pertaining to quantitative analysis. It does not follow, however, that the data are therefore less adequate, but only that the criteria for the evaluation of its adequacy are less easily agreed upon. In dealing with the problems of inference and proof in qualitative research, Becker points to certain similarities between quantitative and qualitative analysis:

> In assessing the evidence for such a conclusion the observer takes a clue from his statistical colleagues. Instead of arguing that a conclusion is either totally true or false, he decides if possible, how *likely* it is that his conclusion about the frequency or distribution of some phenomenon is an accurate quasistatistic, just as the statistician decides, on the basis of the varying values of a correlation coefficient or a significant figure, that his conclusion is more or less likely to be accurate.[13]

C. THE INTERVIEW

The most critical problems facing the interviewer have to do with reliability and validity. By "reliability," I refer to the consistency of the data and its amenability to replication. By "validity," I refer to the accuracy or truth value of the data.

Methodologists generally agree that validity and reliability are seldom both maximized in any one interview situation, particularly when the interviewer wishes to probe at some depth. In such situations, it seems some compromise must be accepted. Despite the generally unstructured nature of my interviews (necessary for purposes of

13. H. S. Becker, "Problems of Inference and Proof in Participant-Observation," *American Sociological Review* 23, no. 6 (December 1958): 656.

validity), some systematic controls were built into the study design in order to enhance reliability. First, the focus of the interview was concrete and specific—"How did you go about committing such-and-such a criminal act?." Secondly, various dimensions of behavior (for example, temporal, technical, and social organization) were systematically inquired about. An interview guide developed in terms of these dimensions was referred to near the end of each interview. I would point out to my respondent that, in order to ensure that I would not forget anything, I would like to go over my list of items. These would then be read to the respondent. If omissions were noted, we would pursue their correction. Frequently, although the topic had been dealt with earlier, its rephrasing as an item on the interview guide would elicit additional comments by the respondent.

Cicourel considers the use of systematic controls inadequate both for reliability and validity. He points out that "Each interview will not exist again for eliciting the properties called data." [14] He emphasizes the fact that the interview is a social situation and that its success depends on the adequacy of the system of meanings shared by the two participants. To the extent that this system of shared meanings varies between any two persons, standardization militates against reliability. In this sense, then, "reliability cannot be achieved by the same procedures for all subjects, but only for each subject taken separately." [15] The answer, as Cicourel sees it, is to make explicit the system of shared meanings, and to take them into account when interpreting the data. He correctly points out that our present knowledge, both of systems of shared meanings and of the ways of studying them, is inadequate, as also is our knowledge of how this inadequacy may affect the data.

This problem is particularly difficult in a study such as this, which has as one of its foci the very systems of shared meanings Cicourel talks about. In this sense, the interview becomes both the method and the object of study. In part, Cicourel's caution is taken into account by the socialization period that preceded the formal inception of this research.

The two most persistent criticisms directed toward prison research focus on the representativeness of the prison population of criminals in general, and on the validity of the material gathered. I have dis-

14. Cicourel, *Method and Measurement in Sociology*, p. 81.
15. Ibid., p. 80.

cussed the problem of representativeness. The validity consideration may stem in part from the prevailing myth that the prisoner
is without moral restraint and not to be trusted, plus the knowledge
that the prisoner has been involved in activities that he has an interest in keeping secret.

Those acquainted with prisons would add that in order to gain
approval of custodians for possible parole, the prisoner may find it
necessary to put on an act or play the role of someone he isn't, nor
has been. Negatively, it may take the form of exaggerated criticism
and imputed mistreatment. Whatever its form, this digression from
"reality" is referred to by custodians as "the con line." The assumption seems to be that any prisoner can, if he wants to, take on this
role. It is also assumed any prisoner is an expert in determining
when and when not to use the con line. Parole officers' casual conversation centers heavily around the clues by which they learn to
separate "fact from fancy."

Prison administrators, correctional officers, as well as the inmates
themselves, continually warned me to beware of the "snow job."
Several inmates said something to the effect that, "I suppose a lot
of the guys are just giving you a line?" My reaction to such a query
was to appear gullible, rather than to indicate mistrust. I felt in
no position to engage in the battle of wits that I so often saw in
parole officer-parolee interaction. I quite simply stated that I felt
my respondents were being very helpful. I had indicated to all of
them that, although I could, I did not wish to read their official
files, and preferred to base my study on their statements. In other
words, I began on the premise of trust and I believe this expecta-
tion was met. I suspect there was some exaggeration in the form of
over-dramatization; it is probable that, in the retelling of biographical events, some aspects now seem to be more significant than they
possibly were at the time of the event. This, of course, is a problem
not unique to prison interviewing.

My project could be thoroughly and openly discussed with the inmate; nothing needed to be hidden. The nature of the research and
the reasons for it could be discussed without reservation. Furthermore by asking "how," instead of "why," I was giving recognition
to the skills they had developed. Placing their skills within the
general rubric of work and occupations implied continuity rather
than discontinuity between themselves and myself.

Most subjects felt they had little expertise on skills to offer. In fact, they did not easily associate the concept "skills" with illegitimate activity. A number expressed surprise at the association. In contrast to what my many "advisors" from custodial and correctional staff had told me, I met with a great deal more modesty than I did with the exaggeration of skills. Perhaps this was because of my initial imputation of skill, or because I was expressly interested in examining these "often exaggerated" skills, in contrast to most interviewers who are basically interested in discovering deficiencies of various sorts. Their defensive reaction was toward my expecting too much of them, rather than too little.

Validity was assessed by internal checks (biographical consistency and attention to detail) and external checks (the use of files and observations of others). Several independent measures of validity were used:

1. Prison and agency files were used, wth the subjects' permission, whenever internal checks (such as biographical consistency) implied that the data were invalid.
2. For numerous subjects, cross-checking with a partner's story was possible. Subjects frequently suggested I ask someone else about certain details of which they were uncertain. Such cross-checking provided opportunity to assess the validity of responses.
3. Referrals made by parole officers frequently included short introductions: for example, "He's done a lot of holdups," or "He's never done anything big, but he knows what he's doing." Also, casual conversation with correctional staff, and overhearing their comments regarding certain inmates provided additional external checks on the general validity of the data.
4. Methods of opening safes and of dealing with burglar-alarm systems were also discussed with safe manufacturers and with a large detection service. Their comments, on how to foil the criminal were in harmony with what the criminals told me. Clearly, the perspectives were different, but the technological issues were similar. For example, a senior member of a safe company asked me, "I suppose they [the criminals] tell you they can open safes just by turning the dial and feeling for the right combination?" I replied that none had claimed such ability. "Well, if they ever do, you know it's not true—today's safes simply can't be opened that way!"

Each subject was encouraged to relate the details of several capers he had participated in, and to choose such capers that, when retold, could not possibly have legal repercussions for himself. In addition, each subject was encouraged to select at least one caper that was successful, and one that was not successful. Their choices indicated what the criminal considers to be success or failure within his own occupation. The unsuccessful cases were also useful in bringing to my attention aspects that had been overlooked in descriptions of successful capers.

Becker has suggested that qualitative research would become more "scientific" and less "artistic" if the data were presented in "natural history" fashion. This would require ". . . presenting the evidence as it came to the attention of the observer during the successive stages of his conceptualization of the problem." He stresses that the reader be given ". . . greater access to the data and the procedures on which conclusions are based." [16]

The format of this research is based partly on Becker's advice. The natural history of the research has been outlined; the reader, moreover, is given access to much of the data. Many quotations are included in order to assist the reader in his assessment of the analysis.

16. Becker, "Problems of Inference and Proof in Participant-Observation," p. 660.

BIBLIOGRAPHY

Back, K. W. "The Well-Informed Informant." In *Human Organization Research,* edited by R. H. Adams and J. J. Preiss. Homewood, Ill.: Dorsey, 1960.

Becker, H. S. "Problems of Inference and Proof in Participant-Observation." *American Sociological Review* 23, no. 6 (December 1958).

———. *Outsiders.* New York: The Free Press, 1963.

———; Geer, Blanche; Hughes, Everett; and Strauss, Anselm L. *Boys in White.* Chicago: University of Chicago Press, 1961.

Brown, R. *Explanation in Social Science.* London: Routledge & Kegan Paul Ltd., 1963.

Bryan, J. "Apprenticeship in Prostitution." *Social Problems* 12, no. 3 (Winter 1965).

Camp, G. M. "Nothing to Lose: A Study of Bank Robbery in America." Ph.D. dissertation, Yale University, 1967.

Cavan, Sherri. *Liquor License.* Chicago: Aldine Publishing Co., 1966.

Chubb & Sons, Lock and Safe Co. Ltd. *Too Late!* Leicester: Scepter Litho. Ltd., n.d.

Cicourel, A. V. *Method and Measurement in Sociology.* New York: Free Press of Glencoe, 1964.

———. *The Social Organization of Juvenile Justice.* New York: John Wiley & Sons, Inc., 1968.

Clinard, M., and Quinney, R. *Criminal Behavior Systems: A Typology,* New York: Holt, Rinehart & Winston, Inc., 1967.

Cloward, Richard. "Illegitimate Means, Anomie, and Deviant Behavior." *American Sociological Review* 24 (April 1959).

Cressey, D. R. *Other People's Money: A Study of the Social Psychology of Embezzlement.* Glencoe, Ill.: The Free Press, 1953.

DeBaum, Everett. "The Heist: The Theory and Practice of Armed Robbery." *Harper's* 200 (February 1950).

Dubin, R., et al. *Leadership and Productivity*. San Francisco: Chandler Publishing Co., 1965.

――――. *Theory Building*. New York: The Free Press, 1969.

Einstadter, W. J. "The Social Organization of Armed Robbery." *Social Problems* 17, no. 1 (Summer 1969).

Garfinkel, Harold. "Conditions of Successful Degradation Ceremonies." *The American Journal of Sociology* 61 (March 1956).

――――. *Studies in Ethnomethodology*. Englewood Cliffs, N.J.: Prentice-Hall, Inc., 1967.

Gibbons, D. C. *Changing the Lawbreaker: The Treatment of Delinquents and Criminals*. Englewood Cliffs, N.J.: Prentice-Hall, Inc., 1965.

Glaser, Barney G., and Strauss, Anselm. *The Discovery of Grounded Theory*. Chicago: Aldine Publishing Co., 1967.

Goffman, Erving. "On Cooling the Mark Out." *Psychiatry* 15, no. 4 (November 1952).

Gold, Ray. "Janitors versus Tenants: A Status-Income Dilemma." *American Journal of Sociology* 57 no. 5 (March 1952).

Goldstein, Leon J. "The Phenomenological and the Naturalistic Approaches to the Social Sciences." In *Philosophy of the Social Sciences*, edited by M. Natanson. New York: Random House, Inc., 1963.

Hall, Jerome. *Theft, Law and Society*. Indianapolis: The Bobbs-Merrill Co., Inc., 1952.

Hughes, E. C. "The Sociological Study of Work: An Editorial Forward." *American Journal of Sociology* 57, no. 5 (March 1952).

Irwin, John, and Cressey, Donald. "Thieves, Convicts, and the Inmate Culture." *Social Problems* 10, no. 2 (Fall 1962).

――――. *The Felon*. Englewood Cliffs, N.J.: Prentice-Hall, Inc., 1970.

Jackson, Bruce. "Who Goes to Prison." *The Atlantic* 217, no. 1 (January 1966).

――――. *A Thief's Primer*. New York: The MacMillan Company, 1969.

Letter to the Editor. *Playboy* 16, no. 8 (August 1968).

Martin, J. B. *My Life in Crime*. New York: Signet Books, 1952.

Maurer, David. *The Big Con*. Indianapolis: The Bobbs-Merrill Co., Inc., 1940.

――――. *Whiz Mob*. New Haven: College and University Press, 1964.

Merton, R. K. "Social Structure and Anomie." *American Sociological Review* 3 (October 1938).

Polsky, Ned. *Hustlers, Beats and Others*. Chicago: Aldine Publishing Co., 1967.

Roebuck, J. B., and Cadwallader, M. L. "The Negro Armed Robber as a Criminal Type: The Construction and Application of a Typology." *Pacific Sociological Review* 4 (Spring 1961).

Roy, Donald. "Quota Restrictions and Gold-bricking in a Machine Shop." *American Journal of Sociology* 57 (March 1952).

Sacks, Harvey. "Notes on Police Assessment of Moral Character," in *Studies in Social Interaction,* edited by D. Sudnow, New York: The Free Press, 1972.

Schelling, Tomas C. *The Strategy of Conflict.* Cambridge: Harvard University Press, 1963.

Schur, Edwin. *Crimes Without Victims,* Englewood Cliffs, N.J.: Prentice-Hall, Inc., 1965.

Shaw, Clifford. *The Jack-Roller.* Chicago: The University of Chicago Press, 1930.

Skipper, J. K. and McCaghy, C. H. "Lesbian Behaviour as an Adaptation to the Occupation of Stripping." *Social Problems* 17, no. 2 (Fall 1969).

————. "Strip-teasers: The Anatomy and Career Contingencies of a Deviant Occupation." *Social Problems* 17, no. 3 (Winter 1970).

Skolnik, J. *Justice Without Trial.* New York: John Wiley & Sons, Inc., 1966.

Sudnow, David. "Normal Crimes: Sociological Features of the Penal Code." *Social Problems,* 12 (Winter 1965).

————. *Passing On.* Englewood Cliffs, N.J.: Prentice-Hall, Inc., 1967.

Sutherland, Edwin. *The Professional Thief.* Chicago: The University of Chicago Press, 1937.

Thomas, W. I. *The Unadjusted Girl.* Boston: Little, Brown and Company, 1923.

Thrasher, F. M. *The Gang: A Study of 1313 Gangs in Chicago.* Chicago: University of Chicago Press, 1927.

Turner, Roy. "Occupational Routines: Some Demand Characteristics of Police." Unpublished paper presented to the Canadian Sociology and Anthropology Association (June 1969).

Vollmer, Howard, and Mills, Donald. *Professionalization.* Englewood Cliffs, N.J.: Prentice-Hall, Inc., 1966.

Whyte, W. F. *Street Corner Society.* Chicago: University of Chicago Press, 1943.

Williamson, Henry. *Hustler!,* edited by F. Lincoln Keiser. New York: Avon Books, 1965.

Wiseman, J. P. *Stations of the Lost.* Englewood Cliffs, N.J.: Prentice-Hall, Inc., 1970.

Wolfgang, M. E., and Ferracuti, F. *The Subculture of Violence.* London: Tavistock Publications, 1967.

Zilboorg, Gregory. *The Psychology of the Criminal Act and Punishment.* New York: Harcourt Brace Jovanovich, 1954.

INDEX

O

Ohlin, L. E., 24
Organizational skills, 4–6, 49, 92–107, 117, 164
Overt crimes, *see* Armed robbery; Bank robbery

P

Peeling (safecracking technique), 77–78
Penal classification, 14–18
Penitentiaries Commission, 38
Perceptual skills, *see* Casing
Perspectives on criminality, 13–48
    contrasting lay and criminal, 19–40
        basic distinctions, 20–26
        criminal as prisoner, 37–40
        professionals and amateurs, 26–32
        specialization, 32–36, 42
    legal criteria and penal classification, 14–18
Petty theft, 26, 36
Pickpockets, 5, 165
Police, 41–48, 84–86, 115, 148–49, 154–56
Polsky, Ned, 3, 4, 67
Prairie Penitentiary, 38
Prisons, 37–40,
    as schools of crime, 122–30
Professionalism, 26–31, 159
Prostitutes, 8, 24
Punching (safecracking technique), 78

Q

Quinney, R., 30

R

Reckless, Walter C., 30
Recognition, 41–48

Reformatory experience, 118, 120–21
Reputation, 41–48
Robbery, *see* Armed robbery; Bank robbery
Roebuck, Julian, 164
Rounders, 20–22, 26, 28, 31, 38, 42, 130, 161

S

Sacks, Harvey, 149
Safecracking, 6–7, 35, 37, 43, 56–86, 91, 116, 129, 134, 136, 169–70
    casing, 138–39, 141–45, 147, 151, 154–55
    techniques, 66–86
        gut shot, 74–75
        harnessed safes, 76
        interpreation of, 79–86
        jam shot, 68–73, 75–76
        nonexplosive, 77–79
        shooting for space, 73–74
    technological change and, 87–89
    tools, 58–66
        detonators and fuses, 64–66
        nitroglycerine, 58–63, 65
        soap, 63–64
    types of safes, 57–58, 66–67, 74, 87, 88
Schelling, Thomas C., 148
Schutz, Alfred, 10, 11
Shaw, Clifford, 2, 165
Shooting for space (safecracking technique), 73–74
Shoplifting, 36, 163
Simmel, Georg, 10
Skills, *see* Mechanical skills; Organizational skills; Social skills
Skipper, J. K., 8
Soap, use in safecracking, 63–64
Social skills, 49–50, 108–16, 164
Specialization, 32–36, 42, 87, 129, 159
Square-johns, 20, 22, 161
Sudnow, David, 5, 15